The Ultimate Plan for Success

God's Original Purpose for Your Life

Author: Charles Boampong Kodom

Copyright © 2019 by Charles Boampong Kodom

Unless otherwise stated, all Scriptures used in this book are quoted from the New King James Version.

All rights reserved. No part of this book may be reproduced or transmitted in any form without written permission from the author. The use of Scriptures, quotations and certain pages for personal or group study is however permitted and encouraged. In such an instance, a few pages may be copied for the success of the group discussion.

ISBN

EBook   :   978-0-620-82543-6

Paperback   :   978-0-620-82531-3

For more information, contact:

charlso2016@gmail.com or letty.calbert@gmail.com

+2783 976 2008 / +2760 338 0406

DEDICATION

I dedicate this book to everyone who is ready to cause a positive change to society, nations and the world at large. To all people who are so tired of life and have tried everything possible yet failed, I dedicate this book to you and to announce to you that your star has appeared so get ready to cause changes. To anyone who says, I really want to understand God better and experience His love for myself and family, I dedicate this book to you. I want to personally present this book as a free gift to you from God. God has sent me to offer you deep mysteries about Him that can provide answers to all your questions. With your faith and determination, I can see your life changing already. Take your time as you read through the pages and meditate on every detail.

Meet you again soon with great testimonies…

 **Thumbs up!**

FOREWORD

God the creator of heaven and earth; and all that is in it during creation had a unique plan that influenced His decision to create the heavens and earth and eventually put a man in charge to manage everything.

There was a time I was in a state of confusion; when I looked around nothing seemed to make sense at all. Why are human beings going through certain difficult situations, where there seems to be no solution coming from anywhere? Meanwhile, when I read the Bible it states categorically clear that God has solutions for all our problems. All we need to do is to ask Him for help and He is more than ready to come to our aid and provide the solutions we're looking for. After several prayers without the needed solution coming forth, one day I finally became bold enough to ask the question "why did God even create us in the first place?" If God had not decided to create us, there wouldn't be any sufferings, pains, sorrows and even hurting God Himself since we tend to do that every day through our various bad deeds.

As humans, we battle with so many issues in our minds and even in our daily lives which influence us to ask ourselves so many questions, as I was doing at that time. Dear reader, if you find yourself in a similar situation, then this book" The

Ultimate Plan for Success" answers it all. It explains vividly the reasons why God created us, the beautiful life (the life in Eden) and the successful life He wants for us.

It further indicates how one can re-discover himself or herself after sinning; not to allow Satan the 'master evil- schemer' to confuse and entice one to continue sinning. He (Satan) makes it seem like when one sins, there is nothing like re-discovering yourself or it is almost impossible to move out of sin to become a better person and live in conformity with the biblical principles. It shows God's readiness to embrace us with open arms to His bosom to continue with His ultimate plan of creating us. Inasmuch as we battle with issues of depression, poverty, disappointments, the death of loved ones, stagnation, etc.; all the above mentioned are demons related and spearheaded by Satan himself just to make our lives miserable and win us to his kingdom.

It is never God's intention for us to suffer or go through difficult moments. God's main plan is for us to become successful and experience a fulfilled life, but Satan plans the exact opposite for us! It is hence not surprising to me when I look around day by day, I see people who are busily working hard and tirelessly to make earns meet or to become successful in life one day, but they still remain in the same place. Although certain people are sometimes influenced by

Satan and through their own personally motivated schemes, they use dubious means other than what God expects of them to become successful.

This book is a must-have book that highlights all aspects of life from various perspectives – biblical, social, motivational, etc. It is not just any book, but a book written by the author who is no other than my best friend, motivator, advisor, my other half, a gift from God to me as a husband. A man who nothing excites other than the Word of God and things related to the Kingdom of God. God has given him a lot of revelations, inspiration, and motivation to write this spirit-filled book just for you and the entire world to know that His reason for creating the heavens, the earth and all that we see in it including man was never a mistake or without special purpose to excel.

Dearest reader, whatever you need to be in life, that is being successful and also to live a life that will enable you not to miss heaven at the long run is all inscribed in the 'Ultimate Plan for Success'.

May the Almighty God bless you as you keep on reading and receive all the revelations you need to become the person God created you to be.

MRS. LETICIA FORJOUR KODOM

Content

- Preface   1
- Introduction   4
- A Prophetic Prayer and Declaration that will change your life for good   11

Chapter 1	The Purpose of Creation	14
Chapter 2	Life in Eden	39
Chapter 3	Missing the way	59
Chapter 4	God's saving grace and restoration	74
Chapter 5	Rerouting-How to get back to God and inherit your possessions	82
Chapter 6	Your relationship with God	96
Chapter 7	Who are you?	110
Chapter 8	Dominating the Earth (divine calling)	132
Chapter 9	Remain faithful onto God – Intimacy with God	163
Chapter 10	Simple Life Model of Success	207

Preface

It's been decades since God Almighty handed over some special keys of life to me. I made lots of effort to understand what each key meant to me and what specific role they played in my life. In the quest for that, I received another message that exposed me to how God's children are suffering in this age because of the lack of revelation in His Word. The Holy Spirit dropped in my spirit that everything we're currently looking for on earth is already found. It was the first time the Bible verse that says, 'God can do all things' made sense to me. This also taught me that reading or hearing the Word of God without the presence of the Holy Spirit cannot make a difference in our lives. This is why we have many Bible Scholars and Professors in Theology who believe in the Bible but do not exercise the power in the Word regularly to cause visible changes. The Bible says, "*the Word became flesh*" (**John 1:14**). I want to bring you to the level of understanding that when the Bible says, "*No weapon formed against you shall prosper*" (**Isaiah 54:17**), then God really means it. It is not a matter of mere theory or religious saying. We have a huge problem in the Christian circle, where many people believe that God can do all things, yet they don't trust God enough to cause His promises to come to pass in their lives. If for example, a Christian sister prays for someone to rise from the dead, a common reaction that one may experience is: the people around her may think that the miracle cannot possibly be true; it must be some sort of trick or charms. Such a comment is usually passed by the church first before non-Christians join. I'm only citing this as an example of one of the common challenges that the church is facing today, and due to that, we are not able to see much of the power of God compared to the days of old. Besides, it is stated clearly in **John 14:12**, "*Most assuredly, I say to you, he who believes in Me, the works that he will do also; and greater works than these he will do, because I go to My Father.*" This means that if Jesus raised the dead, then we can also raise the dead and even do more. We make it appear like God is not powerful enough to cause certain changes in our lives. This is an error that will be corrected after reading through this book. The main focus of this book is to inform you that God holds the answers to everything and that He made you in a very special way such that you and God will make the best team that can achieve anything that you may desire in life.

Introduction

I thank God Almighty for the lives of all people who have been favored by God to be alive today because of the special grace which God has released to His children in our generation. The Bible says knowledge shall abound in the last days and the Spirit of God shall fill all His people. It also says in **John 4:23**, *"But the hour is coming and now is when the true worshippers will worship the Father (God) in spirit and truth; for the Father is seeking such to worship Him."* We have lived in the dark for many centuries, even in the days of the early prophets because the knowledge and revelation of the Word were hidden from the lives of people. The Bible says, *"hearing they will hear but they will not understand, seeing they will see but they will not perceive; for the hearts of this people have grown dull."* (**Isaiah 6:9-10**). Many Christians have the wrong conception that salvation is the only journey for a child of God. Some Christians believe that their sickness or poverty or struggles or challenges in life are caused by God in order for them to remain as faithful Christians. I believe that salvation is the first step to acquire in a Christian's journey. This means that after receiving and working towards your salvation, there are many other good things that this salvation offers you: good health, long life, riches and wealth, peaceful life, deliverance and breakthrough, love, children and family, miracles, signs and wonders, holy life, divine protection, etc. Unfortunately enough, many Christians ignore all the other benefits of salvation and only concentrate on the salvation of their souls because of the lack of understanding of God's true intention for creating man. What they fail to understand is that the absence of certain necessities in life can lead you into sin and cause you to lose your salvation in the end. For example, some people may be lured into corruption and prostitution with the sole aim of raising enough money to take care of their families. The Bible says we must feed the poor and take care of the oppressed and those who are persecuted in society. The question is if you are poor yourself, how can you take care of the poor or defend the oppressed? You obviously will not use a physical fist to protect the oppressed, you will need money to pursue their rights and provide them with the necessary security measures.

I'm exceedingly glad that God has chosen to reveal the mysteries of His Kingdom to this generation because He said in His Word, *"I shall pour out my spirit on all flesh; your sons and daughters shall prophesy, your young men shall see visions..."* (**Joel 2:28**). We live in days where God is doing mighty works through great men and women of God like the days of the Apostles of Jesus Christ. Today, God has given me the grace, wisdom and mandate to reveal some hidden mysteries to many of His children in the world by publishing this book as a free gift to the world to set God's children free, as well as to give them the answers that they have been looking for all this while. I want to advise my readers that this book is not just an ordinary book or story or history, but this book contains hidden treasures in heaven that provide solutions to real-time problems here on earth. There is a huge reward that awaits us on earth, even before we go to heaven. It is written in **2 Corinthians 8:9** "*For you know the grace of our Lord Jesus Christ, that <u>though He was rich, yet for your sakes He became poor</u>, <u>that you through His poverty might become rich</u>.*" But the question is why are people still struggling either spiritually or physically? It is a practical book, which when applied well can restore your relationship with God, restore your family, restore your finances, deliver you and your family, bring about the promotion that you are looking for, bring healing to your body, grant your business and career breakthrough, etc.

I, therefore, recommend this book for everyone: young and old, rich and poor, men and women, employers and employees, Christians and non-Christians, etc.

If you have ever asked yourself one of these questions, then this is the right book for you:

- How can I maximize my potentials?
- How can one gain financial freedom and take absolute control of everything that surrounds them?

- How can one experience a high performance at work, school or any environment they find themselves?
- What is God's plan for my life and what does He expect of me?
- Is it okay to remain poor as a practicing Christian?
- What kind of life must one live as a Christian or as a true citizen of a particular country?
- How can I manage my family effectively?
- How can I serve God the right way?
- Can I ever pick up myself and do it right or is it too late with my issue?
- How can I live a fulfilled life?
- How can I overcome all the challenges I'm facing?
- Does God really care for me or know that I exist?

- Why is God not answering my prayers?
- Am I called by God?

Prophetic Prayer And Declaration

In the name of Jesus Christ, the name above all names both in heaven and on earth, to whom you have come before today, I pray for you. The Bible says the Kingdom of God is not a matter of words but of power. It is also written that faith without works is dead.

I pray that the Spirit of the living God who has led you to discover His mysteries from this book will fill you and mount upon you from this day and begin to teach you deep things of God that will perfect all your ways. I pray for the touch of the Holy Spirit wherever you may be, for it is written nothing is hidden before the eyes of the Almighty God.

May He fill you with the Spirit of Excellence to achieve things that you couldn't achieve with your own efforts and intelligence. May the same Spirit that raised Jesus from the dead re-energize your spirit for mighty works. I pray that any demon or evil spirit that has been hindering your works in the past will be disarmed and destroyed from this day forth, for it is written, "every knee shall bow by the mention of the name Jesus Christ." The Bible says, for our sake He came to die a very painful death to take away our sins, poverty, and shame so that we can be saved, blessed and become prosperous. I, therefore, say unto you that all your struggles ended on the cross and you should not suffer a second time because Jesus paid the price for you and I. I pray that the Hand of the Lord shall envelop you; may the perfect blood of Jesus cleanse you from every sin in the past or present that may rise up against your blessings even as you read this book. The Bible says the whole creation has been waiting for the manifestation of the children of God; I, therefore, declare unto you to arise and cause changes in your family and nation as it was said unto Gideon, "the Lord is with you, you mighty man of valor". Beloved it is written that God knew you long before you were even conceived in your mother's womb. I, therefore, say unto you that you shall succeed not by human wisdom or experience but by the Spirit of the Living God; for it was said onto the first man, be fruitful and multiply and dominate the whole earth. Beloved, I want you to understand that you cannot afford to live without causing great and positive changes to your family, nation, and the world at large. I, therefore, pray for you to receive the power to dominate and take over. Receive the power to cause changes wherever you may go in Jesus' name. I believe that you're whole and equipped, ready to cause changes by the Spirit of the living God. In the wonderful name of Jesus Christ, we pray, Amen.

Chapter 1

The Purpose of Creation

Each time God created something from the 1st day to the 5th day of creation, the Bible recorded, "*And God saw that it was **good**.*" But on the 6th day when the man was created, it was recorded, "*Then God saw everything that He had made, and indeed it was **very good**"* – **Genesis 1:31**. Before I leave out something so significant, I understand that God became **very satisfied** after creating man. This means that God was not just satisfied, but He was **VERY (Extremely) satisfied when the man was created**. Even though He found it necessary and good for creating the other things, including all other living things, He became very fulfilled when the man appeared in the scene.

Secondly, it is very important for you to understand that man did not appear out of the blue; God had him in His mind when He started creation. In fact, I can say the man was the core reason why God created the heavens and the earth. This can be confirmed from the verse which was written immediately after the man was created, "Then God **saw everything** that He had made, and indeed it was **very good**." Inasmuch as God was constantly checking every stage of the whole process of creation, right after the man was created, He did a thorough checking (God **saw everything** that He had made) to see that all the components of creation did fit into the main agenda of creation – thus man. Another Bible verse puts it, *"When He assigned to the sea its limit, So that the waters would not transgress His command, When He marked out the foundations of the earth, Then I was beside Him as a master craftsman;*

And I was daily His delight, Rejoicing always before Him, <u>Rejoicing in His inhabited world, and my delight was with the sons of men</u>" – **Proverbs 8:29-31**. We are told in this Scripture that there was rejoicing in the creation of God; but among them all, the delight of God was with the man. It means the man was God's first priority of creation. This basically means that man was created for a special mission on earth. According to an online article published by LiveScience at <u>https://www.livescience.com/32437-why-are-250-million-sperm-cells-released-during-sex.html in 2018</u>, an average male can produce an estimated number of 525 billion sperm cells in a lifetime. It was also said that between 40 million to 1.2 billion sperm cells are released by a healthy man in a single ejaculation. This also means that your birth did not appear by chance. Come to think of it, it means that the probability for you to be born out of the 525 billion sperm cells is, $\dfrac{1}{525000000000}$, which is approximately equal to 0.000000000001904761905 chances of you being born. If you did some Mathematics, you'll understand that your chances of being born were 0%. In other words, you literally had no small chance of being born, yet you have arrived. Do you want to call this a chance? Let me break it further for everyone to understand me: this means that out of the 40 million to 1.2 billion sperm cells that were released to compete on the day that your parents met, you came first and the rest died on the spot. There are two very important things involved in your birth: (1) **divine agreement** and (2) **divine empowerment**. This is to say God intentionally formed you before you were conceived in your mother's womb and He empowered you to take over the world. This means if you were not beautiful enough, God was going to reform you before permitting your mother to conceive you. I'd, therefore, want you to be proud of your beauty, skin color, family background, race or gender. You must also understand that it was a serious competition that took place during the first day of your formation. Even though there was no parental influence involved when your parents met, yet you came out victorious that day and became the ultimate winner. Inasmuch as you had no experience in life and had not been formed fully yet, you still became a winner. My simple question is do you think you can fail now? That's absolutely impossible. I do understand that the births of some people were surrounded by so much tragedy and unpleasant situations but those moments do not mean that you were born by chance. As a matter of fact, God knew that you were coming to the earth even before the conception of you actually took place by whatever means. Can you imagine what the other several million could be doing right now if they were given the chance to come to the earth? Some could probably become renowned Presidents of State, Political Leaders, Professional Engineers, Academics, Medical Doctors, High Court Judges, Lawyers, Police Commissioners, Teachers, Powerful Men and Women of God, Businessmen and women, Scientists, Economists, Renowned Actors and Actresses, Professional Footballers, Billionaires, etc. Now if you can process all this, then you will understand that God chose you because you were more powerful than all of them. In fact, you're the best and perfect by all standards. So I'd, therefore, ask you not to dwell so much on the misery or unpleasant situation relating to your birth (if you ever experienced that at all) and then begin to concentrate on your divine assignment on earth, **Ecclesiastes 12:13** *"Let us hear the conclusion of the whole matter: Fear*

God and keep His commandments, for this is the whole duty of man." To add to this point, the first commandment that God gave man was mentioned in **Genesis 1:26**, which will be discussed in detail later on in this book. In summary, God told the man to dominate the whole creation in **Genesis 1:26**. So even as you read through this book, I'd like you to have it at the back of your mind that you're not a mistake and God knows you personally and has entrusted everything that He created into your hands so that you can dominate all – that is who you are!

To look at it with an eye of revelation, the Bible says God is the Alpha (beginning) and Omega (end) – **Revelation 1:8**. We have also read that God created man in His own image and likeness. These verses sum up to say that **man is the beginning and end of creation**. It is very important to note that everything that God created is subject to man and He has given us the <u>power to start and end</u> anything that we may put our hands in; being it project, work, school, etc. I, therefore, wish to grasp this opportunity to encourage you that whatever project that you started and you have been struggling to finish, God has given you the power to finish it and you shall indeed finish it successfully.

Because of familiarity with life in this world, many people hardly find time to think about or reflect on God's divine purpose for creating a human. Modern society has taught us, right after we're born to begin to map out strategies to combat life's challenges which include: strategies to maintain healthy living, strategies to receive quality education and vocational/technical training, strategies to acquire financial freedom and strategies to lay a good legacy, just to mention a few. All of these are very wonderful things to consider in life if a person wants to achieve their dreams in life or print a positive mark in society. I am very much convinced that every 4 out of 5 people that you may pick randomly to ask about questions of life may provide an answer that encompasses one of the elements that I have mentioned. This means that almost everyone has some sort of vision or plan for their life but the question is how many people are able to achieve their dreams before the end of their useful life on earth? Today we have professors who are greatly distressed because of one problem or the other; we have scholars holding PhDs and Masters who are living hand to mouth sort of life; we have anointed men of God and pastors who are ultimately loved by God, yet are experiencing abject poverty in life; we have psychologists who are facing serious psychological problems; we have legal experts and professionals who are faced with serious household problems in one way or the other; we have big-time business tycoons with so much wealth and are thinking of how to end their own life as we speak; we have very successful people in society who everyone admires, yet they are so much stressed and hold serious grudges against themselves. In a sentence, how will you summarise all that I have pointed out? **JUST HAVE A MOMENT OF REFLECTION AS WE GO THROUGH THE REST OF THE PAGES.**

Have you got any answer(s) yet? Whatever your answer(s) may be, I'm assuming that your conclusion was that there may be a possible problem somewhere that we need to address, even though it may be hidden in a way.

Today, every electronic or electrical appliance that you buy from the shop comes with instructions of use in the form of a manual. This really helps a lot if especially it is your first time of using an appliance of that sort. Even more, if one buys a Samsung product and still finds a problem with it after reading through the manual, he/she immediately call the manufacturer for help. The same thing applies to human beings and their purpose on earth. We are created differently and may have different dreams in life, but there are some underlying objectives common to everyone. Whichever angle that you may look at it, everyone is looking for peace, love, success, good health, growth, promotion, etc. The approach and passion in the field of operation may differ, but we all hope to achieve common goals. In order to achieve our purpose on earth, it is therefore very important to understand our divine purpose from a Biblical perspective.

As it is written:

"Then God said, 'Let Us make man in Our image, according to Our likeness; let them have dominion over the fish of the sea, over the birds of the air, and over the cattle, over all the earth and over every creeping thing that creeps on the earth."

Genesis 2:26 NKJV

I will throw a little light on the first part of this Bible verse and then discuss the second part in the other chapters. At the beginning of creation, God did not discuss with the man that I want to create you man so what's your opinion about that? Just as the manufacturer of Samsung Products felt it necessary to create such products, God also thought it necessary to create man. This means that man had no clue about his purpose on earth until God told him so. This also means that we have no idea about what goes on in creating a human so we also have no right to take away our own lives. No matter how bad things may seem, we must always remember that our ending shall be glorious and victorious as God had planned. (**Jeremiah 29:11** *"For I know the thoughts that I think toward you, says the Lord, thoughts of peace and not evil, to give you a future and a hope."*) In order to understand the purpose of a man from the Creator's perspective, it is very important to understand the nature of God. God said, *"Let Us create man in Our own **image** and **likeness**."*

By referring to the image of God, God was referring to His Majestic and Awesome looks. This confirms the Scripture that says that *"we're fearfully and wonderfully made"* – (**Psalm 139:14**). It is very sad to hear some people refer to themselves as 'nobody' or 'useless' because of some temporary challenges that they may be going through. There is no sickness or deformity in the image of God, and we must be like Him. Jesus said I took the stripes at my back for your healing. Someone may ask, so why do we get sick and even acquire deformity from birth? It is a good question though, but as the Bible puts it in **Isaiah 5:13**, "*my people have gone into captivity because they lack knowledge.*" This means that the dark side of life may come to us, but it takes knowledge and revelation in the Word of God to correct such inconsistency. The Bible says the people of Jericho understood that God loved them, yet their water was bad (**2 Kings 2:19-22**). They saw an inconsistency with the Word of God because the Bible says you shall eat the best from the land and dwell in the land of milk and honey. Through revelation, they consulted the Prophet of God and he prayed and the water was cleansed from that day till now. The question is if they had not got the knowledge and revelation of the Word of God, their water was going to remain bad and kill everyone even though God loved them? Sometimes I feel that the relationship between God and us is like the judiciary system in any country; they say ignorance of the law is no excuse. God has given us the manual for life in the form of a Bible, so it is our responsibility to seek for the knowledge in the Word and understanding. This is exactly what happens to us; we suffer many things, not because we ought to, but because of the lack of knowledge and revelation of the Word.

In order to understand the likeness of God, we need to look at the common attributes of God: **He is the Creator**, meaning God has endowed each and every one of us the power to create things. I mean everyone can create something useful to benefit mankind. In the business cycle, we only train certain people with some special skills if only we are preparing them to take over some special assignments and roles. For God to say, let us create man in our own likeness, then it simply means He was preparing the man to take up the things He started in the beginning (**1 John 4:17**, "...*as He is, so are we in this world*). So God built something like a big empire, which had big-time businesses, investments, treasure, people and everything in it and asked the man to manage it. This is why it is not good to remain idle because God knew the temptation in remaining idle, which will be discussed later. This means that besides the spiritual glory, a man is born very wealthy in terms of material things. If for some reason you cannot find the wealth and glory that God gave you, then you must know that the devil has stolen from you and for that reason you must fight and claim them immediately. Many Christians actually don't see anything wrong if you are not financially okay, but I want to tell you a hard truth that **everything is wrong for a Christian to live in**

perpetual lack. Even Apostle Paul said in **3 John 1:3**, "*Beloved, I pray that you <u>prosper in all things</u> and be in health, just as your soul prospers.*" He made it very clear that it is necessary to prosper in **ALL THINGS** as a Christian. I like it when he indicates that your general prosperity (ALL THINGS) should be directly proportional to your spiritual prosperity (SALVATION OF YOUR SOUL). All things mean every aspect of your life must flourish and bear fruit. So I don't know where some Christians got the idea that it is okay to remain poor.

Actually, the Bible explains in **Matthew 25:14-30** about the Parable of the Talents,

- that a man gave out five talents to one of his servants, to another, he gave two and to another he gave one as he was preparing to travel to a far country. The Bible says the men who received the five and two talents had invested their monies and managed to double the initial

*amounts. However, the one who received only one talent just hid his money and did not do any investment with it. The Bible says after a long time the lord of those servants came and settled accounts with them. When those two who invested their monies made their accounts, their lord said, Well done, good and faithful servants; you were faithful over a few things, I will make you ruler over many things. Enter into the joy of your lord. Then he who hid his money and made no investment returned the same money that was given him. But his lord said to him, <u>You wicked and lazy servant</u>. He then commanded them to take away his talent from him to be given to the one who managed to get more talents. And the Bible concluded with the words, "**For to everyone who has, more will be given, and he will have abundance; but from him who does not have, even what he has will be taken away.**"*

What actually comes into your mind when you read the above Bible account? Unless you're holier than God, then you can say their master was not fair with the one who was given one talent. As a matter of fact, the most confusing part is when their lord commanded them to take from the one who didn't do anything with his money and give to the one who had more. In the natural sense, one would think that their lord was going to feel sorry for the one who had little and even add some more talents to him because the others were already doing okay. But unfortunately God does not operate like that; we serve a principled God whose ways are far different from our ways. I have seen many young and energetic Christians putting on sad faces, moving to and fro around the church during very busy hours of the day when their colleagues are so busy making good money from work. Dear reader, if you don't find yourself in this picture, please kindly pass on the message to someone you know because many Christians (not all) are being destroyed because of laziness and the lack of knowledge. We need to save their lives. Another shocking lesson to take from the account is that as the people rendered accounts to their lord on what was given them, each and every one of us will render an account about what we did with everything that God endowed us with. **This means many poor people will be judged for their poverty because God didn't plan for them to be poor in life**. That means you wasted the resources that God endowed you with because if those resources were given to someone else, the person could have multiplied them. So I want you to quit folding your arms and start making plans that can transform your life, family, and community. And lastly, **God will never add more to you when He finds out that you are not**

doing anything with what He has already given you. Many people are given great talents, skills, and opportunities but they are doing absolutely nothing with them and they are now busy in the church praying and fasting. You have been praying for ten years on the same issue and nothing is happening. Sometimes your prayers may not be answered not because of demons fighting your answers like the case of Daniel, but it could be that you already carry the answer that you are looking for, and all you need is knowledge and direction. Most of the poor people we see around are billionaires in the sight of God, but they're busy blaming God for their situation and blaming even the people around them. Arise as a giant, seek the face of God the right way, ask for wisdom from above to do things well and put your hands into something good and the Lord will bless you. I'd also like to mention that **we are all called by God to**

be a solution to the world, so you must strive by all means to become what God wants you to become in order for you to fulfill your divine calling. The failure of one man is not just going to affect that one person but it can affect a whole nation. Imagine if Moses had died as a child, then the Israelites could have remained in slavery for far too many years. **It is God's intention for man to lack nothing**.

Martin Luther King Jnr once said, *"You must fly but if you can't fly, then you must run but if you can't run, then you must walk but if you can't walk, then you must crawl; but whatever you do you must try at all means to keep moving."*

The Bible also says in **1 Peter 1:15-16** *"but as He who called you is holy, you also be holy in all your conduct, because it is written, "Be holy, for I am holy."* This confirms the Scripture that says we are a chosen generation, a holy nation and a royal priesthood (**1 Peter 2:9**). This means that we're called onto holiness and moral living. As Christians, we are supposed to be the light of this world; but we see the opposite today. The church has thrown away all its values and now copies almost everything that the world offers. People are now shy to talk about Jesus in the workplace, school and public places because of conformity with the world's standards.

My own assessment tells me that about 90% of the world's population believe that God created human beings, whether Christians or non-Christians. If this is the case, then it is very essential for man to remember that he cannot get everything done right on his own, except by consulting the manual for creating him (which is the Holy Bible) or his Creator (God Almighty). What is your personal take on this analogy? I personally think it is only proper to consult God or the Word of God to define our true purpose on earth. Since one can consult an equipment's manufacturer or the manual for proper and effective use of the equipment, then we should be quick to consult God for answers concerning life. Is your life not more valuable than the expensive cell phone that you just bought? How amazing it is to find a person spend a whole day or week or even month to read carefully the whole manual of the newly bought extravagant phone and yet fail to have his morning prayer in a whole week. Of course, it is a very good thing to read instructions carefully before the use of any item; but I am bringing the issue of your own life as a whole that if your phone deserves such kind of care and attention, then you as a person deserve even better.

What or who do you consult when defining your purpose in life? Maybe you consult career experts, psychologists, family, friends, pastors, mentors, teachers, books, past experience, etc. to help you define your purpose in life. These sources can be very good, especially when you are a little confused. On top of these sources, you need a true blueprint sourced from the Creator's own perspective of your life as the first and most important thing to do before the other sources can impact you positively. God created you as a holy man or woman, a very successful person, a winner, a wealthy and an influential person, a solution bearer, a person who can cause positive changes in their family, community, country or world, and on top of it all, to be able to represent God in a positive manner.

Chapter 2

Life in Eden

Have you ever wondered about the sort of life Adam and Eve experienced in the Garden of Eden? Just to give you a brief highlights, the Bible says they were surrounded with gold and precious stones (**Genesis 2:12**). Beautiful flowing rivers running through the garden at all seasons; natural vegetation with different kinds of plants, trees, and animals was just too nice to behold. Have you ever thought of how rich Adam was? God actually gave him everything that He created. Not only did God give him authority over all living things but He also gave him the power and ability to create things and cause changes at the same time. As a matter of fact, he called all animals to himself one after the other and gave them names as he wished. This means that the authority that God gave him was so much that it gave him sufficient protection and glory that no lion or any kind of wild animal could scare or harm him. I strongly believe that Adam could talk to the animals and plants and they could hear and obey him. Not only that, the Bible says that Adam spoke with God on daily basis, and it is also written that God is Spirit and no man can see His face physically. This means that Adam's spiritual senses were so sharp and active that He could discern the presence of God each time He came down to the Garden.

If there's anything that I have desired on earth, then the first one must be a desire to have the Eden's experience before man sinned against God. It gives you a clear picture of God's initial plan for man and the kind of power that He gave him. It is also important to understand that man was created as an immortal being and could not die for whatsoever reason. If this could be the case in our time, then it can only mean that man was given authority over every sickness or disease e.g. Cancer, Hypertension, HIV/AIDS, Heart Problems, Hepatitis, Paralysis, Liver Problems, Skin Diseases, etc. Not only that, imagine if you experience a severe car accident or a plane crash and you cannot die, then what sort of creature are you? This means that man could possibly appear and disappear any time; man could possibly fly; man could possibly hear and see literally everything within his surroundings without having to move his physical body to all those places, etc. In other words, man possessed special systems within him which included a satellite that monitored everything within his surroundings. This means that man had very sophisticated senses and systems to do all things but we lost them. This is so amazing to know. Now if you are wondering, my question is have you ever been able to define or describe God fully to explain everything about Him? No one can, and the Bible says as God is, so are we. With those abilities, one could communicate with anyone anywhere in the world without the use of any mobile technology. Man could appear in different places at the same time within microseconds. These are facts that we ought to know as Christians, which the devil obviously doesn't want us to know. Ask yourself, how many places or countries are being influenced by Satan right now? How many people are being possessed and manipulated by Satan right now? So many, you may guess. Even if Satan could have these abilities, then how much more man, who was made in the image and likeness of God? In fact, a man possessed more complex capabilities than these modern computers and even robots that we see in movies. At least you will understand why I've always desired to have the Eden's experience. In fact, the Bible calls Jesus the second Adam, which means the first Adam was made to be exactly like God Himself. As we speak, we have many people who love nature and desire to develop some intimacy with certain kinds of wild animals, but because of the high risk involved, they'll not dare. In fact, Adam had the privilege to be with all these wild animals and they all recognized him as superior and untouchable. He could play with a lion any time he felt like. God could have created many people at the same time but He only created Adam and Eve, hoping that they would reproduce (create) many offspring.

The Bible says in **Genesis 2:15** "*Then the Lord God took the man and put him in the garden of Eden to tend and keep it.*" To start a sentence with 'then' means that there was a preceding act which led to the latter one. To quickly summarise, God had just planted the beautiful garden called Eden before He created man. When God finished planting the garden, He then knew that man was ready to come to the earth because the systems to sustain him were already in place. I have heard people say they are alone in this world and there's no kind of help coming from any quarters to support them and that's the main reason why they are not making it in life. That is a wrong way of thinking because this verse just said God prepared the garden before creating Adam. This is to say before everyone is born into the earth, there's already a garden prepared by God Himself for you to take over, tend it and keep it. Thus your own houses, cars, businesses, luxury, etc. are provided by God even before you are born. This is a deep secret and hidden truth that applies to every human irrespective of your race, gender, social class, health situation or educational background. This confirms the Scripture that says before you were formed in your mother's womb, I knew you (**Jeremiah 1:5**). Does this verse answer the question: Am I born by chance; whether through a very unpleasant circumstance or not? Please keep yourself very well and always remember that God has a very special assignment for you and He believes in you more than anybody else on earth. People may not believe in you and may even judge you, but rejoice because they don't know better than God, Who created you. Our own Bible tells us that God does not make mistakes; which means you and I can never be a mistake: whether male or female, black or white, short or tall, etc.

Now it is more convincing that the kind of abilities that God gave us is beyond human comprehension. One day I was reading the Bible and I came across **John 20:21-23**, "*So Jesus said to them again, "Peace to you! As the*

Father has sent Me, I also send you." And when He had said this, He breathed on them, and said to them, "Receive the Holy Spirit. <u>"If you forgive the sins of any, they are forgiven them; if you retain the sins of any, they are retained</u>," I screamed after reading it, especially the last part where Jesus gave us the authority to forgive or retain sins. Can you believe this? If only we knew the things that we could do, our lives were going to be too sweet. Let me quickly share with you the interesting story of Esau. The Bible says God loved Jacob but hated Esau (**Malachi 1:2-3**). We also read that it was Jacob who received all the blessing from his father Isaac and Esau received more or less nothing to live on or a curse to serve his younger brother Jacob. Because Esau understood the purpose of a man on earth, the Bible says he worked very hard until he became wealthy in a way that he built a city of his own called Edom.

Sometimes when people read the Bible, they just run through it and are not able to understand the main message in today's context. Considering the total population of the world at that time, I can say building a city could be compared with building a whole province or nation in our days. The Bible says when Jacob offered gifts to Esau, he refused them and said: "*I have enough my brother; keep what you have for yourself*" (**Genesis 33:9**). This is the main reason why even non-Christians are able to use certain godly or Biblical principles in life and become very successful in their business and other areas. It is therefore very important for you to know that you have no excuse to remain poor in life; unless it was a choice you made yourself. Maybe you didn't know, but I want you to understand that it is not a good thing for a Christian to be begging for things or borrowing always; it is an insult to our God. I will, therefore, urge you to begin to concentrate on your abilities, rather than your weaknesses or failures.

Coming back to the verse, God gave the man the responsibility of tending and keeping the garden. Whatever position that you may be occupying in your workplace, God expects you to be fruitful and keep the business running with the best of your abilities. You are planted in a particular office for a special assignment, no matter how small your position or business may be. I've seen people purposely refusing to give their best at work because of dissatisfaction at the workplace but I call that self-cheating. Do you think that Joseph could leave the prisons if he had not given his utmost best? He served faithfully and helped everyone in the prison, even though he didn't deserve to be there. He didn't allow bitterness to hold him backward, but instead, he served God faithfully through men. Some people allow bitterness to take over their entire souls and chase them away from their destiny because they couldn't handle their unpleasant situation with maturity and revelation. It may be true that you must have been treated unfairly but one thing you should understand is that the ways of God are not the ways of men. Sometimes God can use something so disgusting and humiliating to promote you so you must be more sensitive to the voice of God, and not the pains that people may afflict on you. Do you think Lot could have been saved from the fire if he had acted on emotions when he met the Angels? To give you a clearer picture, the people of Sodom and Gomorrah were so much evil and wicked that no one would dare open their door to anyone, let alone a stranger but Lot saw the Angels with another eye, welcomed them and even brought them to his house (where he had two virgin daughters) just to take care of them (**Genesis 19:1-3**).

What a risk! This is how God rescued Lot and his family. Please don't make decisions based on emotions or by the fact that you are hurt. My sister or brother, you need to have this eye that sees beyond the present situation in order to tap into some blessings.

Another important thing to remember is that life in Eden requires high spiritual sensitivity to survive. This is the life of affluence, power, and authority. Everything in the garden looks so nice and flashy that it can easily cause you to be tempted to be making decisions in a carnal manner because of beautiful looks. The Bible says *"Eve saw how beautiful the fruit was..."* (This will be discussed later). Do not be enticed with everything that looks nice in your eyes when God starts blessing you. Many have been led to their grave because of the quest for what looks so good in the eyes, without first considering the possible consequences or finding out from God if it is His will for them to possess such position, item or anything that you can think of.

The last point that I would like to talk about is how to deal with your family life. Family life is so important that there is not one single person who can completely say that he or she is not connected to someone in any way. You may be connected to someone as a family by blood or through friendship. God instituted the family system when He first brought Adam and Eve together and gave them the ability to reproduce more of their kind. There are many things that are required in maintaining a family, but I'd only address one important component that is required to maintain a healthy family. **Every great family is built on love**; it is the main foundation of a family. People in a family are willing to sacrifice anything to help the people they care about most. This was the same thing with Adam and Eve. However, there is one big problem where people compromise to everything that their loved ones propose to them without thinking twice. Many youths are suffering today because their parents failed to correct their wrongful acts at their tender age; their parents probably applied the concept of love wrongfully, thinking that the act of correction or rebuke could mean the lack of affection or love. Adam could have saved himself and even his wife if he had done certain things. I said earlier that it is not good for a person to remain idle. Whether young or old, male or female, we were all created to be doing something constructive all the time so please find yourself a good job to do as husband and find a modest job for your wife also to do at all cost. Don't say you earn more than enough so she should just sit in the house and watch movies, you may regret later. To husbands, no good man can stay idle for a year; that will mean suicide. Do something even if no company is employing you. Think about something to do at all cost; even if it means voluntary sweeping of the streets of your township, it is still a good job. Many people find the perfect excuse for staying idle when no company is employing them.

Secondly, when Eve fell into the trap of the Serpent, Adam could have resisted and save himself and probably pleaded with God for his wife; which I'm sure God could forgive and spare her life. But he carelessly took the fruit from her, all in the name of love and ate it. Anything that your partner may do contrary to the will of God is evil; it cannot be love. The Bible says true love hates evil but we rather accommodate both good and evil all in the name of love.

"Love suffers long and is kind; love does not envy; love does not parade itself, is not puffed up; does not behave rudely, does not seek its own, is not provoked, thinks no

evil; does not rejoice in iniquity, but rejoices in truth; bears all things, hopes all things, endures all things. Love never fails."

1 Corinthians 13:4-8

From the Scripture above, love does not think evil and does not rejoice in iniquity. This means true love rebukes evil. If your husband comes to you and tells you that he loves you too much and for that matter he's going to get you the latest Rolls Royce within one week from his share of a fraudulent deal that took place at work, look at him in the face and tell him, "my king, my lord, and my warrior, get behind me Satan; I am not a party to evil so you can keep your dirty money to yourself." For that moment, he'll be swimming in a pool of confusion trying to put all your contrasting words together to make sense. This was what Adam was supposed to do. I want you to understand that **any act of love that claims to love**

more than the love of God is of evil origin. Let me quickly tell you what King David said when his wife tried to come between him and God:

"Then David returned to bless his household. And Michal the daughter of Saul came out to meet David, and said, "How glorious was the king of Israel today, uncovering himself today in the eyes of the maids of his servants, as one of the base fellows shamelessly uncovers himself!" So David said to Michal, "It was before the Lord, who chose me instead of your father and all his house, to appoint me ruler over the people of the Lord, over Israel. Therefore I will play music before the Lord. And I will be even more undignified than this, and will be humbled in my own sight."

2 Samuel 6:20-22

King David stood firm by his belief and rebuked Michal, his own wife for disrespecting God just because she saw him worshipping God in public. Never allow your wife or husband to disrespect God in your presence. Adam could have done exactly what King David did but he compromised and allowed his wife to take the place of God at that moment because if he had thought about the fear of God, he wouldn't have listened to Eve. Your wife can't tell you to come into her on a Sunday morning when you have to prepare to go to church and worship God. The moment you hear such requests, you must know that it is no longer her talking so you must rebuke the demon responsible for that.

We are told from the first Scripture that love does not seek its own. I always say if you are married, see your partner as your only child who is so dear to your heart. Now if you have ever had the experience of having a dear child, you'll understand that everything that you'll do in life will be because of him or her. Sometimes when you are too weak and sick and don't want to go to work, the moment the thoughts of him/her comes into your mind, you immediately look for your bag, forget about your sickness and begin going to work. This is all an issue of making sure that your child lacks absolutely nothing essential for their wellbeing as long as you're still alive. We need to think of our partner in a like manner. The Bible actually says we should think of our partner more than we must think of ourselves. This is a secret that if you are able to live by, there will be nothing that could be so strong to crush your marriage.

Another important lesson from the verse is the part that said love bears all things. This means there's absolutely no situation that true love cannot handle. However big the problem with your wife or husband may look like, love can handle it. Often times, people ask themselves, what will people think? We don't marry because of people's opinions about certain decisions we make in our marriage. It is not an issue of who can take this? It an issue of whether you want to take it or leave it? And what is influencing your decision? Is it of God or of man?

Chapter 3

Missing the way

"for all have sinned and fall short of the glory of God,"
Romans 3:23

A man was created in a very special and glorious way by God to take exactly after Himself. God gave a man the powers to represent Him and take decisions on His behalf. This special relationship between God and man was broken because of sin. In **Genesis 3:1-6**, the Bible explains how man sinned against God and lost the glory of God which he carried before. Had it not been the sacrifices that Jesus Christ, our Lord, and savior made for us, then Christians were going to remain in eternal slavery. Sin stripped us naked and left us empty. A man was created to operate as a spiritual being, with very sharp spiritual senses. Adam was able to communicate with God and the entire creation because of his spiritual abilities which God gave him. He had the power to command the sun, the moon, the stars, the earth and everything in heaven above and on earth below and even to create anything he so wished either by a spoken word or by craft. To break it further for you and make it easier for you to understand in plain language, death was subject to Adam. The spirit of infirmity (or sickness), the spirit of poverty, the spirit of divorce, the spirit of delay, the spirit of failure, the spirit of rejection, the spirit of stagnation and the spirit of lack were all subjects to Adam. This means he ruled over these spiritual forces that destroy man, and none of them could affect him until he sinned. So I'm sure you can now understand the extent of loss that he suffered when sin entered him. This is also true for every other human being on earth who sins against God. When you sin and remain in the sin, you give away your inheritance and birthright as a child of God. Sin opens many doors in your life for demons and all kinds of troubles to enter in your life. In the spiritual realms, God has put a hedge of protection on every child of God, so what sin does is that it breaks this hedge of protection surrounding you and then exposes you to all forms of attacks. Sin actually starts in a very small and cunny way. You fall into the pit of sin when you accommodate the enticing words that the devil may propose to you. For this reason, it is very important for you as a child of God to stay out of trouble and live the godly way without any form of compromise. Don't say you have the Holy Spirit so you cannot fall into a certain kind of sin or trouble. The moment you open up your doors to sin, you immediately grieve the spirit of God living in you. The Bible says light and darkness cannot coexist and one cannot serve two masters at the same time. God is holy so once you allow sin to get close to you, you disrespect Him and make Him incapable of providing His protection to you because you've brought in a new boss. That's why the Bible says resist the devil and he'll flee. This means that the devil will always come to look for the opportunity to destroy you, but it will take you to decide whether you want to accommodate him or ask him to go away with his nonsense. Dear reader, I want to tell you that it is a wrong thing to try to negotiate with the devil; you owe him no explanation or anything else as a child of God. Now the Bible says:

"And he said to the woman, has God indeed said, 'You shall not eat of every tree of the garden'?"

Genesis 3:1

Look at the verse closely and so many questions will pop up in your mind. Why did he go to the woman and not the man? Why did he not initially speak about that particular tree which God said they must not touch? Why did he have to bring God into the matter and did not talk about the personal decisions of Eve? Why did the devil act like he and Eve were friends long before and asked her intimate questions about her private life? Are there more questions coming into your mind?

What Christians don't know is that the devil has a special department in hell whose main objective is to package all forms of sins, test them and then present them to Christians in a very attractive way so that Christians can fall into his trap. I'm quite certain that Eve did not think about the depth of the question asked by the Serpent and probably took it as a normal question. Dear reader, the devil always comes in a much-disguised manner that you'll not suspect anything until you have drunk deep into sin. Each time the devil comes to you, he first casts a spell to weaken you so if the protection on you is not strong enough, then you must be in trouble at that moment. This is the reason why Jesus said, pray without ceasing, because you don't know what time the devil will come to you. Apostle Paul even said, what I don't want to do are the things I do, and what I do are the things I don't want to do (**Romans 7:15-20**). This means that the devil can cause you to make decisions that you wouldn't make when you are in your right sense of mind.

1. Why did he go to the woman and not the man?

You must probably be thinking that the woman is the weaker vessel that's why the devil chose to go to her, but I will be discussing this issue from a different angle. I'd like to briefly talk about gateways to sin. Gateways are strategic entry points which the devil uses to enter a person. In the dark world, the devil has a big factory that studies the activities of every Christian and discovers loose spots that he may use to enter that person. When he finds out that you're spiritually active, he will then begin to look for gateways that could take you by surprise. So when the devil realized that it was going to be very difficult to deal with Adam, he then decided to get to him through Eve. In fact, Adam was the main target, not Eve. This means that when the devil wants to attack you, he does not come for the branches, he looks for the roots to destroy, which will, in turn, destroy the whole plant. You must understand that if you're a praying woman and your husband is not, then the devil may use your husband as a gateway to get into you and vice versa. I am tempted to think that the time that the Serpent visited Eve, was a moment when she was idle. Eve was literally doing nothing at that time of the day;

she was probably doing her makeup and admiring her beauty. Adam must have been busy somewhere in the garden so the devil decided to take advantage of the moment (Satan does not miss an opportunity). There's, therefore, the need to avoid being idle. Even when you're not doing active work, you can engage your mind in prayer or brainstorm on some ideas.

2. Why did he not initially speak about that particular tree which God said they must not touch?

The devil knows that if he goes straight to the point, you will find out about his hidden agenda so he may ask a very provocative and general question that will cause you to react without thinking. For example, if you are a very successful couple and a journalist asks the question: so did you get married to your wife because of her wealth and social class; just to give you a boost in your political pursuit? I can tell you that many people can answer this type of question first before they even think about the question. They may answer on impulse in an attempt to refute what the enemy is saying against them. You are not obligated to speak immediately when a question is asked or if you're irritated with the question or if the question looks too simple and straight forward; you might have been set up to fall into a trap. **One of the most difficult things to do in life is to learn how to control your emotions and learn how not to answer back when you feel offended and humiliated unfairly**. Don't get too distressed about people's wrongful opinion and negative comments about you, stay focussed and do what you know best even the more. Don't lower yourself to their level by trying to fight back verbally; let your good works speak.

3. Why did he have to bring God into the matter and did not talk about the personal decisions of Eve?

You must be careful with people who come to you and talk about what other people are doing or have done in a bad way. I'm not saying that each time a topic is raised concerning someone else, then it must be of evil origin. I am only aware that gossips sometimes use that approach so you should be able to discern which one is of good intention and which one is not. One of the things that many Christians don't know is that we're currently enjoying privileges from heaven, that not even the Angels of God, or Satan and his demons got the privilege to enjoy. The Devil desired to be like man so that he could enjoy the special grace that God gave man but because he could not become like man, he then plotted to cause man to sin so that man could be demoted from his glory just as he was first stripped naked from his privileges as an Angel of God. Now when the devil realized that there was a problem between him and God, he also thought it necessary to cause a problem between man and God. Unfortunately enough, Eve did not know anything about the Serpent and his past, so she started pouring her heart out until the devil pushed her to the corner. Please be very careful with people and act wisely each time you want to talk. The Bible says this tongue that we see although very small, yet it has the power of life and death.

4. Why did the devil act like he and Eve were friends long before and asked her intimate questions about her private life?

Do not get over yourself too quickly when people appear to be too nice to you, or act like they care for you and are interested in your matter. They might be spies and probably be looking for information to destroy you so don't sell yourself to them so cheaply. When people raise very sensitive and private matters about you, without you necessarily inviting them for such kind of discussions, then it is only proper for you to probe further to know their main motive before you even utter a word.

Let us quickly look at a major trigger to fall into temptation:

*"So when the woman **saw that the tree was good for food**, that it was **pleasant to the eyes**, and a tree **desirable to make one wise**, she took of its fruit and ate. She also gave to her husband with her, and he ate."*

Genesis 3:6

We will look at two important actions that took place and as a result lured the woman into the trap of the serpent. The Bible says the woman **saw** that the tree was good for food. Until I explain it, you may not understand the true context of this word 'saw' as used in the verse. It means that after the devil spoke with those enticing words, the woman then meditated in her heart how nice it would be to become wise. So even as she was seeing the tree, in her mind she was seeing the beauty of the fruits of that tree and what she could derive from it if only she could take a bite. The main thing about meditation is that it ushers you into another realm that you begin to operate in that realm. So seeing just the tree with a considerable amount of meditation then ushered her into a realm of **desire**. This is confirmed by the Scripture which says that if you intently look at a woman and lust after her in your heart, then you have already committed adultery (sin). She came to a conclusion within her heart that the fruit of that tree was all she needed at that time so she began to yearn for it. In other words, the main outcome of meditation is conception and a possible birth. So you must be selective with the things that you meditate on in order to give birth to a good thing. At this point, if the Devil had asked her to buy the fruit at a very high cost, she would do it because her soul and mind were already drawn into it and there was no turning back. This is why the book of Proverbs tells us to keep away from the flattering tongue of a seductress woman and do not lust after her beauty nor let her allure you with her eyelids because you cannot take fire to your bosom without burning your clothes (**Proverbs 6:24,25,27**). This means once you are bitten by the **poison of seeing and desire**, you lose your mind and the devil now tells you what to do. This is why the Bible says in **Psalms 1** that "*Blessed is the man who does not walk in the counsel of the ungodly nor stands in the path of sinners.*" It means that as a Christian, the moment you lower your guards and begin to accommodate anything which is not in line with the ways of God, you begin to contaminate your soul and eventually end up on the other side. It is therefore very important for you to learn how to train yourself as a Christian not to compromise with anything which is not from God because you can be caught unaware by a little slumber. You have to define what you watch and hear (or listen to) as a Christian because they have a great impact on your soul and spirit. Someone will say it's just a song – there is nothing like that my sister, you have to be selective in your choice of songs, otherwise they will destroy your soul. The Bible says that *"Don't you know that your body is the house of the Holy Spirit?"* Eve wouldn't have fallen into the trap of the devil if she understood what she was permitted to look and whom she was supposed to listen to as a Christian.

Chapter 4

God's saving grace and restoration

When you love someone so deeply and for whatsoever reason, the person falls from your hand, you don't stop caring for them, rather you pray for them. The Bible says that if we (humans) as wicked as we are know how to give good things to our children, then how much God, our heavenly Father who loves us unconditionally? – **(Matthew 7:12)**. The Bible explains that one can give away what they love most in order to save a dear one, but to give away your life to save another is something so difficult, yet God sent His Son Jesus Christ to die for us when we were still sinners.

When a man condemns you, it can be forever but God easily forgives our sins. Once the judge in the high court of any state condemns you (after you've made several appeals and tried everything to plead not guilty), there's nothing that you can do about it even if you were innocent. To make matters worse, you are even deprived of certain privileges that other citizens can enjoy when a criminal case is placed against your name. You may not be allowed to hold some diplomatic positions or head some government departments if you have a criminal record. His compassion makes everything different for us. The Bible says:

"For God so loved the world that He gave His only begotten Son, that whoever believes in Him should not perish but have everlasting life."

John 3:16

This is one of the most popular verses in the Bible but today I want you to think about the measure of sacrifice God did for us in a real sense and get a new revelation on this Bible verse. Many people today are burdened with severe depression due to unforgiveness. Some are holding grudges against their partners who disappointed them, others are holding grudges against their parent(s) who did not provide the necessary care for them when they needed it, others are holding grudges against their own children due to disobedience, others are holding grudges against their colleagues or superiors at work, others are holding grudges against their political opponents, etc. All these cases have led thousands of people all over the world to suffer from depression which is seriously affecting them, yet they are not willing to let it go. At a high degree, most depressed people are willing to take hard drugs and even commit suicide but when you ask them to forgive, they tell you that it is so difficult to forgive. This apparently means that many are willing to give up their own lives as long as they are not going to forgive someone. I don't know about your personal experience concerning this matter, but from the little that I know, unforgiveness is a very big problem for many people, if not everyone.

We cannot appreciate what God, through His Son Jesus Christ did for us if we don't take time to analyze how much we struggle to forgive our own neighbor whom we did not create. The second scenario is for us to consider a person you love to death betraying your love. I mean a person that you'll literally do everything for him/her, even if it means you suffering the consequences later. This person could be your close relative, your partner in a relationship, your best friend, your spiritual father/son/mentor, your teacher/student, your most loyal servant, etc.

Even if the people in these scenarios came to apologize, many will still not forgive. But the case with Jesus was so different and awesome. The Bible says from all creation, man was God's favorite. But when man sinned, God became so sad and disappointed in man. But the strange thing is that even at the first moment that God found man in sin, He sewed a cloth from animal skin to cover man when He saw the man naked. For this reason, He gave man His own name and kingdom. What amazing love is this? Today, many people will leave you to die or even curse you to die after you have betrayed their love. We hear cases where a husband shoots his wife for promiscuity or adultery and vice versa. God pronounced judgment on man, but not the one meant for destruction, otherwise, He could have wiped out the whole generation of humans and appoints another living creature as the next of kin. Whilst we were still sinners, arrogant and rebellious, God Himself felt sorry for us and saw the need for Him to personally pay the price for our sins. Have you ever felt sorry for your neighbor who sinned against you or you felt disgusted towards him/her? I'm not trying to convince you but you can't tell me that this act of love which God showed us was a normal thing. As a result, He requested of His Son Jesus Christ to give up His throne and come down as low as our level, suffer humiliation and die to pay the ultimate price for our sins. Can you tell your only son to give up his rights to your laborer or enemy? **PLEASE HAVE A MOMENT OF MEDITATION BEFORE YOU CONTINUE.**

It wasn't so simple like that even when Jesus accepted the challenge to die for us. The most painful thing is that in an attempt for Jesus to pay the price so that man could be restored to his former glory, He was rejected by the same people He sacrificed His life for, even until this day. The Bible says, *He came to His own but His own accepted Him not* (**Mark 6:4**). Just imagine you caught your husband having an affair with another woman and the husband of that woman beat him up mercilessly and locked him up in jail, so you went to bail him, brought him home, treated his wounds, gave him food until he became conscious again. Guess what? When he regained his strength, the first question he asked was, where is my lover? I want to go back to hold her in my arms because my witch wife is now useless to me. This is exactly how we treat Jesus and even worse.

I'd like to say that Jesus came to die for all who believe in His name. You're not too wicked or sinful to qualify. As a matter of fact, no sin is so big before the eyes of God that He cannot forgive. All you need to understand is that Jesus died just for you. And all you need to do is to ask Him for the forgiveness of your sins, accept Him as your Lord and personal savior and be willing to walk with Him in holiness. God has given all of us a second chance through Jesus, the second Adam so that we can be restored to our first glory which He gave us before in the Garden of Eden.

Chapter 5

Rerouting – How to get back to God and inherit your possessions

From the previous chapter, we just read about the perfect sacrifice that Jesus did for us. This reminds us of the stories of how many nations fought for their basic human rights and independence. History has taught us about how the founding fathers of our nations fought so hard to liberate their nations from all forms of oppression, both internally and externally. We all get excited and inspired to hear about historical figures like Abraham Lincoln, Martin Luther King Jnr, Nelson Mandela, Dr. Kwame Nkrumah and many more. They gave up their lives and family just for the total liberation of their people. What I want to bring across is that after sacrifices, comes liberation and fulfillment in life. This means that **there is absolutely no reason to pay a**

price if there is no reward. Interestingly enough in our case, someone paid the price on our behalf and He's giving us an invitation to receive the benefits of His sufferings. The Blood of Jesus has been speaking from the day Jesus Christ died until now. The Bible says the blood of Jesus Christ speaks better things than the blood of Abel (**Hebrews 12:24**). We also read in the Bible that Jesus Christ is interceding for us at the right hand of the Father. This blood which was shed on Calvary is pleading with God the Father to show mercy on us and to forgive all our sins. It is very true that the wages of sin is death (**Romans 6:23**). We sinned against God and we were supposed to be punished for our sins, but Jesus Christ came in the scene to negotiate on our behalf. Jesus came to replace the death that we were supposed to receive with life in abundance. So He is our Mediator and Advocate (**Hebrews 12:24**). Jesus is giving an invitation to all of us to come to Him and lay before Him our burdens so that He can ask the Father to receive us back. All we need to do to receive Jesus is to **acknowledge that we have sinned** against God, to **repent from our sins, confess to God** for the forgiveness of our sins and to **accept Jesus Christ as our Lord and personal Savior**. Later on, I will talk about the enormous blessing, wealth, power and authority that Christ gives us if we receive Him in our lives and how to activate them. However, it is very important to understand the steps that I have just mentioned in order to receive Christ wholly. These steps can be broken into 4 important points:

1. **Acknowledging that you have sinned before God.**

I thank God for His Son Jesus Christ; without Him, we wouldn't qualify to become children of God. He paid the ultimate price to restore everyone who accepts Him as their Lord and personal savior back to the Father. However, you cannot get back to God, without first acknowledging your sins. It is very important for you to do an introspection of your whole life and see where you went wrong. In practical terms, one wouldn't need a physician if his health is in excellent condition. God cannot save you if don't realize that there is something missing in your life, and consequently needs to be fixed.

2. Repentance from your sins

The next important thing to do after acknowledging your sins is to make a decision to move away from them. Repentance from your sins is a key requirement for your salvation. Your sins cannot be forgiven by God until you make the decision to let go your past and accept a new life in Christ because the Bible says one cannot serve two masters at the same time (**Matthew 6:24**); you may either choose to serve the living God or Satan. You do not have to only desire to receive Christ and yet live in sin, you have to genuinely repent from your sins and be willing to start a new life in Christ.

3. Confession to God asking for the forgiveness of your sins

Realizing that you have sinned against God is not enough for your sins to be wiped away; so the moment you become conscious of your sins and be ready to stop sinning, the next action to take is to go before God and confess all your sins asking for forgiveness. Some people only confess on their lips about the sin they committed but they don't make any decision to repent from their sins.

4. Accepting Him as your Lord and personal savior

The last but not the least step is by accepting Jesus Christ as your Lord and personal savior. From this moment, Jesus becomes the boss of your life. The Bible says if anyone comes to Christ, he becomes a new creation, the old things are gone and all things have become new (**2 Corinthians 5:17**). This means that you will no longer live the sinful life that you used to live anymore. This is confirmed by the words of Apostle Paul that, "*it is no longer I who live, but Christ lives in me; and the life which I now live in the flesh I live by faith in the Son of God, who loved me and gave Himself for me.*" (**Galatians 2:20**). I have seen some churches and individuals who say they believe in God but they don't believe that Jesus Christ is the way to their salvation. Unfortunately enough for them, the Bible says the only name, both in heaven and on earth that can save man is the name of Jesus Christ (**Acts 4:12**). This means that you cannot please God without Jesus Christ. Accepting Jesus Christ as your Lord and personal savior is not a one day act of confession but it is a step of faith where you translate your beliefs into action e.g. you don't become a Christian and still remain a liar. We then live a life that will please God but not us or anyone else. The Bible says Christ is the bridegroom and we are the bride. This means that though we were on our own when we were in the world, once a person comes to Christ, they must put all their attention on Christ. Many Christians do a lot of sacrifices in the service of God, yet they are not able to maintain the full standard that Jesus has given us to follow in their Christian life; they still hold onto one or two sins which they are not ready to let go. It is very important to note that one has to surrender completely everything to God. The Bible says we died with Christ and rose with Him. Since Christ died to sin, it means that we also must be dead to sin.

All these four steps are very important and must be done if you really want to see the results of your new life in Christ.

The Bible says, "*all have sinned and fall short of the glory of God*" – (**Romans 3:23**). This Bible verse is telling us that sin is the only thing that strips us of the glory of God which He once gave us. In other words, the only justifiable reason for a permanent limitation in our lives is a sin. This means that it is useless for a holy person to suffer from a permanent limitation. When we turn around, we see many Christians who are living holy lives, and yet remain in poverty. Unless it is a matter of personal choice, otherwise, you cannot be a child of God and still remain poor. I do understand that many churches do encourage their members that as long as you live a holy life, it is not a problem even if you are facing serious financial challenges. This is a very bad doctrine; otherwise, Jesus wouldn't have wasted His time to shed His blood on the cross for us. Jesus said I became poor so that you can become rich. This means that Jesus expects us to be rich spiritually and physically (to be rich in all things). By this, I am by no means saying that a Christian cannot face challenges in life, but I am saying that a Christian must not dwell in perpetual misfortune, because the Bible says in **Psalm 30:5**, "...*Weeping may endure for a night, But joy comes in the morning.*" This is even confirmed by another Scripture that says, "*Many are the afflictions of the righteous, But the Lord delivers him out of them all*" – **Psalm 34:19**. This means that Christians must understand that it is very possible for you to face problems, but one thing that is certain is that you shall come out of all your problems victoriously. That means that every challenge that comes your way is an indication of your promotion. Now God allows us to go through afflictions because He knows that we have been given what it takes to combat every difficult situation in our lives. For this reason I want you to bear in mind that there is absolutely no situation that may come upon you that you cannot solve; so don't accommodate problems for long and accept them as part of your life, arise and fight every unpleasant situation in your life (**1 Corinthians 10:13** *No temptation has overtaken you except such as is common to man; but God is faithful, who will not allow you to be tempted beyond what you are able, but with the temptation will also make the way of escape, that you may be able to bear it*). In essence, every problem that you may face in life already comes with a solution, but you have to first understand this principle and then begin to look for the solution. The reason why many people don't find the solution is that they only concentrate on the problem, which becomes magnified in their eyes and eat them up; but I will encourage you to always look at the brighter side of every difficult situation because He who promised you is faithful. The Bible even says gold and silver belong to God. The Bible goes on to tell us more about fine gold and precious stones in heaven. If these things are bad, why will God keep them? How can the Father be rich and His children remain poor? In fact, any teaching which promotes poverty is demonic. According to the Bible, Abraham, the friend of God and the father of all nations was a wealthy man. His son Isaac was very wealthy. Jacob was very wealthy. The likes of Boaz, Job, David, Solomon, just to mention a few were very wealthy. These were all great men of God who served God faithfully. God said in the book of Genesis, that I am taking you to a land of milk and honey; where you shall lack nothing (**Deuteronomy 11:9**).

The Bible says come to me; all who are heavily burdened, and I shall give you rest. I personally believe that Christians are the most privileged people on earth but we don't know how to use our rights to claim our inheritance.

The Bible says we are co-heirs with Jesus Christ (**Romans 8:17**). Do you know what that alone means? The problem is if we don't preach to people about our faith using our substance and visible evidence, then we make God a liar. We share in His sufferings and glory. This alone tells us that we ought not to remain poor or stranded in life because we share in God's glory. I know that this teaching must be difficult for many religious people, especially if you come from one of the churches who see money as evil. Unfortunately enough the Bible didn't say that money is evil, but it is the love for money which is evil. This means that if your whole life depends on money instead of God, then you're serving money which is wrong. Another person will say but money is the root of all evil. Yes, the Bible says so, but it does not say money is evil. God is only telling us that if you don't learn how to control money, money will control you and lead you into sin. This means that money can become good or bad depending on who possesses it. Don't forget that the same Bible says "money can do all things." The explanation to this Bible verse is quite simple; it means you cannot do anything without money. That is you cannot even go to church without money if there is no fuel in your car; you will not even have a place of worship if there is no money to build the house of God, etc. We, therefore, have to live by example as Christians. It makes no sense for the church to preach to the world about Jesus Christ if we ourselves are not living examples of what God has done in our lives. **Preaching Christ without the manifestation of the Holy Spirit is as bad as noise making.** This is the time to prove to the world that Jesus is alive by bringing the Word to life. If Prophet Elijah called for the fire from heaven in public, then you too can pray for the rain to cease immediately.

Chapter 6

Your relationship with God

In order to understand this chapter very well, I will use the example of the relationship between children and their earthly parents. Except in a few cases, there's always a very intimate relationship between children and their parents in any responsible and loving family. Responsible parents provide shelter for their whole family, they put food on the table daily, they clothe their children nicely, they transport their children to school and many places, they buy gifts for their children, they take their children for excursions, cinema and relaxations, they provide good health care for their children, they provide quality education for their children, etc. These are just some of the things that our earthly parents/fathers do for us. Don't you trust God for these things and even more?

The question is if God, our heavenly father loves us more than our earthly or biological fathers, then are we not supposed to be doing really well in terms of everything as Christians? Yes some Christians are doing fairly okay in life, but many Christians are really struggling: some are in serious debts that they may not be able to pay all till death, some are in serious health conditions, some are struggling to find a simple food to eat in a day, some are barely naked walking in the streets, some are even homeless and sleep in the streets, others are behind bars serving in jails for many years, some are experiencing so many frustrations in their marriages, some cannot even afford to give birth to children, some are failing terribly at work and in school, etc. People get confused when they look at all these things happening to Christians.

For those Christians who are living some sort of 'just survival' kind of life, they may either be renting or owning 3 bedroom apartment, driving an old Mercedes, probably 1990 model, providing some kind of education or training for their children, maintaining some savings worth about $12000 for about 4 years, and a few more. These ones are respectable people who are very hardworking and very forceful, yet they live hand-to-mouth sort of life.

Some people even feel that sometimes it better to be a non-Christian than to be a Christian.

A young girl of about 13 years old, who happens to be one of my students one day in our Mathematics class, asked me this question: "why do Christians suffer so much in life?" I couldn't answer her immediately because the question appeared to me in a shock and at the same time I was thinking about how to package the answer so that she could understand. Of course many people will admit it is a difficult question to answer, especially if you have to explain it to a young person. As she saw me quiet for a moment, she then said I want to be a Muslim now; I do no longer want to be a Christian. Thousands of people share the same concern with this young girl and to make matters worse, heathens even mock and insult Christians for the fact that they also see them struggling even though they are children of the Most High God, the Creator of the universe.

To answer all of this confusion which the devil is using to steal and destroy many of God's children, I would like to first of all say that true prosperity and blessing comes from only God. The Bible says God blessed King Solomon so much that He became the wealthiest man on earth till date. The problem we face today is that we have too many Christians who are serving God from a distance and from a position of no knowledge and no revelation of the God they serve. The Bible says the ways of God are not the ways of men. Most Christians today inherited the doctrine from their fathers as a way of living. It is very important that as a Christian you ought to search for a personal encounter with God. You need a living testimony that will convince you as a person that there is a living God. I'll say don't easily accept when people tell you that God is good and He's very powerful. If you can accept this so easily, then another person can also come and tell you that the moon god is the best and you will quit serving God Almighty and go follow the moon god. Later if another person comes to tell you that the water goddess is the best, you might as well go follow her. So the point is many Christians are frustrated and tired because God is not tangible enough for them. Everything in life that is not tangible and measurable to you becomes boring but the Bible says we serve a living God. **Reading from a book or hearing that 'God is alive' doesn't really make Him alive**. God only becomes alive through our testimonies and the manifestation of His power. Have you felt the goodness and the power of God yourself? Don't wait until you go to heaven before you see the glory of God. I want you to understand that God is looking for serious Christians who can keep an intimate relationship with Him so that He can reveal deep mysteries to them. There is power in the name of Jesus but it's not everyone who mentions the name Jesus can cause changes. Have you tried it before? This means that there is a Spirit that backs the spoken Word. It's not just mere words so we need to have a revelation on that. The Bible says the seven sons of Sceva were beaten up mercilessly by demons because they thought they could copy the ways of God (**Acts 19:14-16**). Beloved many Christians have copied the ways of God and made it a tradition but God is not interested in that. The Bible says on the last day many will come and say we cast out demons in your name but I shall say onto them I do not know you. What does it mean? It means too many people are not worshipping God the right way. **Memorizing the Scripture so well does not make you a believer.** Going to church every day is not the key to please God, praying in tongues is good but knowing God is more than that. Do you feel God when you are eating, sitting, working, sleeping, walking or talking? God is looking for believers who can see Him at all times. Yes it is very possible to build such a close relationship with God, where you talk to Him about everything; like how we relate to our earthly fathers or loved ones. In Chapter 1, I explained the purpose of creation and in Chapter 2, I spoke about life in Eden. One of the reasons why God created us in His own image and likeness is a way of giving us the platform to relate with Him with knowledge and understanding. For example if the Bible says no weapon fashioned against you shall prosper, then you will remember that you were made in the image and likeness of God so if God cannot get broke, then you can never get broke. If the Bible says fear not for I am with you, then you will remember that if God is the Creator of the Universe, then what can scare Him? And this God first of all created you like Himself and secondly He abides in you; so you alone are an embodiment of two Gods- God, the Living One Himself and you because the Bible calls us gods.

The Bible says, *"Blessed is the man Who walks not in the counsel of the ungodly, Nor stands in the path of sinners, Nor sits in the seat of the scornful; But his delight is in the law of the Lord, And in His law he meditates day and night. He shall be like a tree Planted by the rivers of water, That brings forth its fruit in its season, Whose leaf also shall not wither; And whatever he does shall prosper."*

Psalm 1:1-3

When you read this Scripture, does it look like Christians should remain poor or stranded in life? Absolutely no. A pastor comes and preaches this message every day and yet fails to pay his house rent. Does it make sense? The time has come for us to understand that **we need to have God in the inside in order to convert the Word into flesh**. We need to walk in the perfect will of God and then apply faith to the Word. Our generation lacks determination on the promises of God. The Bible says, *"do not give God rest until He answers your prayers"* – (**Isaiah 62:7**). You pray and fast continuously for many days and nights and yet do not see any change in your life so you want to retire from active participation in the things of God. NO, you are a giant in Christ, persevere, do it over and over and over again with knowledge, faith and revelation until God establish you. The Bible says Elijah was a man like us, yet he prayed that there should be no rain and true to his word, for three and a half years there was no rain. **Beloved you need to build an intimate relationship with God so that the whole heaven and earth will know your value. When you reach that level, your voice becomes like the voice of God, so when you speak, Satan trembles and runs away thinking it is God speaking.** The same prophet who prayed for the rain to be held up in the sky also prayed after the three and half years that the rains must now come. The Bible says he prayed and prayed and prayed but there was no rain until the 7th time when a cloud as big as the size of a man's hand appeared in the sky (**1 Kings 18:44**). Do you know why he struggled so much in the second time than the first time? The Bible says whatever we declare on earth is declared in heaven and whatever we establish on earth here is also established in heaven. When the Prophet Elijah prayed that there should be no rain, he did not give a time limit so his declaration changed the seasons of the weather for good. His word became equally as powerful as God's when He was creating the world, so the Prophet Elijah created a new season in the weather that the heavens endorsed. Don't forget that I already explained in chapter one that God created us for us to take over the work of creation from Him; so on the seventh day of creation

God went to rest. He knew the man (Adam) was already in the system to continue with the work of creation and expansion. Now when the Prophet wanted to change the season it became a very big problem for him because it was already established in heaven that there was never going to be rain for a very long time. This is why if you understand the power of words in the spiritual realms, it is so important not to play with words. I am very sure that God felt sorry for the people of Samaria because of the drought; even His own Prophet was affected because there was no water to drink, so God personally told Elijah to go and present himself to Ahab so that He will send rain on the earth. But what happened? Did God immediately send rain after Elijah presented himself to Ahab? No. He allowed Elijah to pray himself seven times until the rain came down. When the Bible says Elijah prayed and prayed and prayed, don't think it was a prayer for just 5 to 10 minutes. We are looking at a minimum of 1 hour for each session; doing the same thing for 7 times (7 hours minimum) without rest. Don't forget his prayer was being backed by the will of God to send rain, yet it was not easy. Apostle Paul said we do not preach empty words, but the words that we speak are of power (**1 Corinthians 2:4, 4:20; 1 Thessalonians 1:5**). I want you to understand the power of words backed by the Spirit of God. Can you also try this in your small village or town, that there should be no rain for only one week? It all comes down to building a deep and intimate relationship with God, where all your ways are ushered by God. Do you think that if a man can call for rain and fire to come on earth at two different occasions, then he cannot change his financial situation? Money must be too simple a thing for him. The

Bible confirms this in **1 Kings 17:8-16**, Elijah prayed for the widow at Zarephath to walk out of poverty.

Chapter 7

Who are you?

By now I am quite sure you're beginning to understand that you're not just a mere human; you are a supernatural being. You were made in the image and likeness of God. Do you know how God looks like? A little picture of His Son Jesus Christ can give you an idea about how God looks like:

"and in the midst of the seven lampstands One like the Son of Man, clothed with a garment down to the feet and girded about the chest with a golden band. His head and hair were white like wool, as white as snow, and His eyes like a flame of fire; His feet were like fine brass, as if refined in a furnace, and His voice as the sound of many waters; He has in His right hand seven stars, out

of His mouth went a sharp two-edged sword, and His countenance was like the sun shining in its strength."

Revelation 1:13-16

Imagine fire came from the eyes of Jesus Christ; from His mouth came a sharp two-edged sword; His voice was the sound of many waters and His countenance was like the sun shining in full brightness. Is there any image that fits this description coming into your mind? Ask a professional artist if he/she can put this description on paper to make one piece? John said I could not look at Him even for a second time. This is exactly how God made you and I (we're fearfully and wonderfully made – **Psalm 139:14**). Evil spirits are supposed to scream and run when they see us. Even though the people around Jesus saw him with their physical eyes, but when the demon-possessed men who lived by the tomb saw Jesus, the Bible says the demons trembled and cried out and said, "*Son of the Most Holy One, have you come to destroy us before our time?*" – **Matthew 8:29**. To prove to you that we have the same features with Christ even though one can only see with spiritual eyes, the Bible says when Shadrack, Meshack, and Abednego were thrown into the lake of fire, the fire could not harm them (**Daniel 3:24**). How is this possible? The Bible says our God is a consuming fire so we ourselves are full of fire; so how can fire burn fire? This is confirmed by the Scripture above when it said "*His eyes like a flame of fire.*" I said earlier that there is a hedge of protection around every believer. This protection is a hedge of fire that scares away evil spirits. The brightness or intensity of the fire differs from one Christian to another. As a matter of fact, every Christian has the responsibility of keeping their fire alive and burning all the time through constant prayers, fasting, studying the Word of God and

Holy living. Many people are attacked and messed up by the devil anyhow and anytime because their fire is low. Keep your fire burning my brother/sister. The book of Daniel also says the hungry lions could not harm Prophet Daniel when he was cast into the lion's den because he carried the image of the Creator. As we speak today, one cannot get near a vicious or crazy dog, let alone to talk about hungry lions. If this happened to a man with blood flowing through his veins like you reading this book, then who do you think you are? The Bible says **all things are subject to men**. The Bible says that when a dead person was brought into contact with the bones of Prophet Elisha, the dead body rose up from the dead (**2 Kings 13:21**). The power in us is too much such that even our dead bones still remain spiritually powerful to raise the dead. Who are you then?

Allow me to highlight on a few things which **Revelation 1:13-16** spoke about. First of all the Scripture described the nature of the garment of Jesus Christ with a golden band at the chest. I was thinking about what kind of garment could possibly have a golden band on one side? We are talking about a very expensive royal costume worth a fortune. It is important for us to understand that as Christians we deserve the best of the best of everything. Our appearance must look very good and decent at all times. You will see a Christian brother/sister dressed in a frayed and out-dated fashion in church on Sunday leading the prayer and worship team. To make matters worse you may find out that this Christian brother or sister is occupying a respectable office at work (financially okay) but chose to dress that way because he/she feels that a prayer warrior or music minister has nothing to do with fashion. If you must inquire more about this person in question, you will also realize that he or she is busy looking for a life partner. The devil has deceived the church for many decades that many Christians still believe that it is even a sin to buy a good cloth to wear because in their own opinion someone somewhere is walking naked. Wake up my Christian brothers and sisters, it is not your fault that someone is in a certain unpleasant situation for you to make your face so sad for the whole year trying to calculate and count even how many smiles you must give in a year. How can we preach to someone that it shall be well if we ourselves are wearing rags? It is not a prayer that you need in order to get a life partner at this point; your main problem is you have made yourself unattractive to suitors and they get scared away. When a Christian brother commends you for your new shoes, you immediately start praying in tongues rebuking him and even stop greeting him because you think he's evil. Apostle Paul said we have fed on milk for far too long so it is time to grow up and act like adults. As a matter of fact, many Christians, including some pastors have made the world unattractive to live in. You will find this priest who is full of the Holy Spirit, who happens to be at the praise and worship service. Even though this priest has been touched so much by the Spirit of God to break out into worship, he turns to the left, right and backward and finds everyone dancing but he holds himself from dancing in public because in his mind priests in his class don't dance in public. You are only allowed to nod your head if the song is hitting you so strongly and sometimes clap your hands in a reasonable fashion for just a brief moment. We must understand that certain practices that take place in the church today are not from God; they are mere human doctrines and this is the right time to break away from such practices that do not glorify God. The Bible says the people criticized Jesus when the woman bowed down to wash His feet with her tears and hair and anointed the feet with expensive perfume. According to the Pharisees, this woman was a sinner and was not allowed to come close to holy men of God but Jesus permitted her to get close to Him. Others also thought that the perfume was so expensive to be wasted at the feet of Jesus; instead, she could sell it and offer the money to the poor. Funny enough Jesus didn't see her sins at that time or did not find the perfume to be too expensive to be used on Him, but He rather saw her sacrifices and was pleased with it. This lesson teaches us that most of the time our thoughts may be completely different from the thoughts of God.

The second thing that I want to talk about on the Bible verse is the part that said: "*His head and hair were white like wool, as white as snow."* This symbolizes purity and holiness. This is confirmed by the Bible verse that says *"We are a chosen generation, a royal priesthood, <u>a holy nation</u>, His own special people..."* – **1 Peter 2:9**. Did you just hear that? Don't give people the chance to say that you are nobody, whereas the Bible says we are God's special people chosen to proclaim His praises. Dear reader, as long as you have given your life to Christ, Jesus will continue to see you as a holy person. You may fall on the way in your Christian journey but that does not make you a sinner. All you need to do is to ask for forgiveness, rise up and continue your walk with Jesus. Sometimes the devil may try to tell you that you are a sinner because of one or two bad experiences you went through in the past. The problem with sin is that the moment you commit the first sin, the devil condemns you in your mind so the next likely thing that can happen to you is that you may accept that you are a sinner and eventually commit a worse sin and continue the trend over and over again. We can confirm this from the Book of Genesis Chapter 4 through the sacrifices that Cain and Abel made unto God. And God said to Cain, *"If you do well, will you not be accepted? And if you do not do well, sin lies at the door. And its desire is for you, but you should rule over it"* – **Genesis 4:7**. God warned Cain that sin was already lingering at his door so he should try to flee from sin and overcome it but he did not heed to the voice of God and ended up committing a worse sin by killing his brother, Abel. Beloved, I want you to understand that no matter how grievous your sin may be, as long as you accept that you have sinned and confess before God for the forgiveness of your sins, you are totally forgiven by God and begin a new life in Christ. All you need to do after Jesus has forgiven your sins is to be ready to live a new life in Christ; don't continue to stay in sin. Make a decision to live a holy life and don't compromise to sin.

Another important message that we can get from the Bible verse above is the part that said: "His voice was like the sound of many waters." I don't know if you have ever experienced the sound of many waters? The closest example that I can give you is the waves and tides of the sea or the sound from a waterfall. This is the type of sound that fills the whole space and appears like some form of volcano reactions are taking place inside the water. It comes with a force. This symbolizes the authority in the speech of Jesus Christ. This is the same authority that Jesus gave to His disciples when he rose from the dead. Jesus gave authority and power to His disciples and said *"whosoever's sin you forgive is forgiven, and whosoever's sin you retain is retained in heaven"* – **John 20:23**. Can you imagine Jesus giving us such great authority? This tells us how much trust God has in us. There is power in our tongue so Christians have to learn how to use their tongue wisely. Confess constantly what you want to become or experience in life and it shall surely come to pass. When the children of Israel were held captives in a foreign land called Babylon, the Bible says there was one particular man who kept on confessing positive things day and night when every other person had given up on God. The Bible says Daniel reminded God that the prophets wrote that the children of Israel were supposed to be in captivity for 70 years, but the period had passed already and they still remained in Babylon (remained in bondage). The point here is Daniel persisted in prayer and confession that they had served their term of 70 years and it was time for them to go back home until

God sent an Angel to bring answers to him. If God told you that your sick sister wouldn't die and she died, what would you do? You may end up giving up on God because you might feel disappointment from your sister's death, which seems contrary to the Word of God. Many Christians miss the point here. I will say a case like this is a clear opportunity for you to exercise your rights as a Christian and experience the power of God. This is where you can put the power of God to work and resurrect the dead. God never promised us that we won't face any storms; instead, He said, He shall be with us in the storms. Why do you think God will appear in your storm or fire or flood moment? He is there only for one reason – thus provide you with answers. But unfortunately enough that is the time that we get so emotional, depressed, disappointed and even end up losing our faith in God. We have to learn to lean completely on the Word of God and nothing else, even if it means death. This is what we call true discipleship. Beloved we have to learn a practical lesson from what the Prophet Daniel did as Christians. Prophet Daniel understood that the promises of God are true and they can never go wrong but you as a believer have a responsibility to enforce the Word to come to pass in your life. To tell you the truth, he never received a direct prophecy from another man of God, but this was a prophecy written in the Bible many years before he was born. All he had to do was to believe and act upon the Word. How many prophecies have you come across in the Bible and moved past them, still expecting God to send someone to carry a message to you face to face before you can get convinced? The Bible says we shall never be the tail but the head. How serious are you taking this Word? It is a prophecy for you and me so don't keep quiet or weep when things are not happening in your life; you need to rise up onto prayer and enforce this Word to come to pass in your life. The Bible goes on to say that we shall lack nothing and our cups shall overflow. But the question is how many Christians are living holy lives and yet find themselves in a situation where they literally beg before they can feed their family? Yet the Bible says we shall live in abundance. Today Christians have given up on God's promises for their lives and now see Christianity only as a necessary social gathering. It doesn't matter how many times you have tried when God says you shall live in abundance, keep on confessing, make room for your wealth, work towards it, live like a wealthy man already and walk victoriously because it shall surely come to pass. The Bible says Jesus prayed in the garden for hours until the sweat on His body turned into blood. Beloved, have you asked yourself what kind of prayer that was? Even for you to pray and sweat, then you will admit that you must have prayed very vigorously for long. This means that the prayer with a sweat of blood is that prayer that you swear in your heart that your answer must drop before you say Amen; otherwise, you would never end your prayer even if it has to take 24 hours. This was the kind of prayer that Moses made when he went up the holy mountain of God for the 10 commandments. Do you think Moses was just sitting down or sleeping for the whole 40 days? No, he was in serious confession, prayer and fasting waiting upon God for His promises. It was the same kind of confession and prayer that the disciples of Jesus exercised in the Acts of Apostles. The Bible says the earth shook when that kind of prayer was offered. Beloved, there is power in our tongue. Another man of God said; if I be a man of God let fire come down from heaven to consume an army of 50 and indeed fire came down to consume all 50. I, therefore, want to encourage you to keep on confessing until you see visible changes in your life, family, and nation. Do you know what happened during the construction of the tower of Babel in Genesis 11? The Bible says they were constantly confessing that they were going to build the tallest skyscraper in the world that would reach the heavens. How do we know this? The Bible says God realized that they were able to do this because they were all speaking a common language (common language means confession of the same thing in agreement). Now the interesting thing is that their confessions were so powerful that things were happening too quickly until there was confusion in heaven and God said let us go down to earth to see what's going on. Do you know the mystery behind the reason why God said let us mix their language so that they cannot understand each other? I know some teachers of the Word have explained that that act was to break the unity between them but I want to give you another revelation on that. To speak different languages does not necessarily require many people but one person can even speak different languages at the same time. What do I mean by this? When you begin to confess that you must buy a private jet, you may have so much belief that it's going to happen. 10 years down the line if it does not happen, you may change your confession to getting a luxury car like Ferrari; however 4 years later if nothing happens, then you be thinking of getting Toyota probably. If care is not taken you might end up going for a motorbike or even a normal bicycle. This is what we call speaking different languages at the same time because of a lack of faith. You may start with a very high faith in the beginning but when challenges start popping up, your faith then begins to shrink and shrink until you lose your initial focus. Many have missed their destinies because of the lack of persistence in confession. So when God mixed their language, the people started doubting their own vision and their confessions changed. The pioneers of the original idea to build the tower to reach the sky started asking themselves questions when they started facing challenges, "do we think we can possibly achieve our aim? Maybe we are embarking on an impossible task." I, therefore, want to encourage you not to change your confessions no matter how hard things may seem.

To add to what I have just explained, the Bible says "out of His mouth went a sharp two-edged sword. We are still talking about the power in your tongue. Do you know what we use a sword for? A sword is used to do many things, especially when the task is beyond the ability of your bare hands. During war, a sword is used to attack and kill the enemy. As you read this book, you are currently facing different warfare in life: financial crisis, marital problems, health problems, emotional problems, spiritual problems, depression, anger problems, stagnation, etc. But the Bible says there is power in your tongue. Begin to confess solution; stop keeping quiet when problems start coming to you. The Bible says, *"For the weapons of our warfare are not carnal, but mighty in God for pulling down strongholds, casting down arguments and every high thing that exalts itself against the knowledge of God, bringing every thought into captivity to the obedience of Christ"* – **2 Corinthians 10:4-5**. We don't fight back physically when people attack us as Christians; rather we go into our closet and begin to confess the solution.

The last thing that I want to share on the Bible verse is the part that said: *"His countenance was like the Sun shining in strength"*. I have already spoken about the fire of protection surrounding every believer but I want you to know that every Christian who carries the Holy Spirit possesses a certain kind of energy around him/her which works like electrical energy. This energy boils within and vibrates around you and handles all situations on your way as you move around. This is why people brought the sick to wait by the side of the road so that when the shadow of Peter is cast on them, they could receive their healing. This is the same reason why many people begin to vibrate and even fall to the ground when some anointed men of God come close to them.

On this note, I would like to say you are a champion in Christ, so great and powerful in all your ways, unbreakable, unstoppable, untouchable and indestructible.

Chapter 8

Dominating the Earth (Divine Calling)

In fact, this is my main motivation for writing this book. For decades and centuries, the church has lost its root and calling to dominate the earth. As a matter of fact, many Christians accept whatever challenge that the world brings them; unlike what the Bible said that we should dominate the earth and everything in it. The picture of the Christian community that I see today can be likened to the message that was written in the Scripture:

"I have seen servants on horses, while princes walk on the ground like servants."

Ecclesiastes 10:7

To tell you the truth the wealth that non-believers are enjoying today is the wealth that Christians are supposed to be enjoying and even more. This is why Apostle Paul said in **Romans 2:24**, "*For the name of God is blasphemed among the Gentiles because of you.*" This is all because we live a completely different life from our calling. I have heard some non-believers pass the comment, "even I (a non-believer) will not do this." Others also think Christians are a totally confused group of people who don't know what to do.

But I am here to tell you that we serve a living and a mighty God. His name is called YAHWEH. The Bible says those who serve God truthfully and in spirit shall bear fruits- fruits that will last forever more (**Psalm 1**). The Bible calls us descendants of Abraham. Since our father Abraham was rich, then as children of Abraham we also ought to be rich. The following account says:

"And the Lord said to Abram, after Lot had separated from him: "Lift your eyes now and look from the place where you are – northward, southward, eastward, and westward, for all the land which you see I give you and your descendants forever. And I will make your descendants as the dust of the earth; so that if a man could number the dust of the earth, then your descendants also could be numbered. Arise, walk in the land through its length and its width, for I give it to you."

Genesis 13: 14-17

This account reveals so many things to us as Christians. First of all, before Abraham could have real-time experience and benefits as a child of God, he had to do certain things. We already know the story of Abraham when God asked him to leave his father's house (because he came from a background that worshipped idols) into a far land which God was going to give him and his descendants. So God separated Abraham from this background of idols. Many Christians have already gone through this process of separation from their past life and dark forces and are now found in the house of God daily; which is a very good thing to do.

Now after Abraham had left his father's house, God started releasing blessings onto Abraham but there was a hindrance because he brought along another family member called Lot. The Bible said even though Abraham had started enjoying a little wealth, but there was serious strife in the house because of the herdsmen of Lot and Abraham. There was no peace in the house because of the constant fights between the workers. So Abraham eventually had to separate with Lot. The Bible says in the above verse that *"And the Lord said to Abram, after Lot had separated from him...... ."* Lot in this context represents any situation which is an abomination to the Lord. Even though you're a born-again Christian, is there any situation in your life that is detestable to the Lord, yet you're still holding onto it? Could it be unforgiveness, gossip, selfishness, greed, anger, discrimination, hatred, lack of self-control, laziness, bad association, or what? There are many things that hinder our blessings and we end up blaming God for our troubles. I cannot judge you and no one can do that either, but I'd like you to search through your heart and find out that hidden and detestable lifestyle of yours which could probably rise up against your blessings and move away from them. It was after Lot separated from Abraham that God opened great blessings from all corners onto Abraham. In fact, the Bible says I give you and your descendants all the land that you see around you; thus northward, southward, eastward and westward. Wow! What an awesome blessing. This is a generational blessing that flows from one generation to the other. The use of the expression 'northward, southward, eastward and westward' is a four-fold blessing signifying blessings coming from all directions – thus blessing in marriage, business, ministry, career, family, school, health, finances, etc. My question is how many plots of land do you have as a child of God? You're still not doing well even if you're having only 5 plots of land by now because that is not the kind of blessing that I saw in the Scripture. When I go back to the Bible, Abraham had cities, gold, cattle, camels, sheep, goats and many more. In those days, the value of a camel was equivalent to the modern cars that we see around today.

One very important lesson that I would like to share with you in the above verse is the part that said, "Arise, walk in the land through its length and its width, for I give it to you." To make it easy for us to understand, let's assume that God was giving Abraham a land as big as the whole land of South Africa. God gave Abraham two important commands to follow:

1. Arise

He commanded Abraham to "arise". The word arise means 'come to light' or 'get up'. Did you notice that until God told Abraham to look at all the four corners of the very same land where he was dwelling, he never caught the revelation that the land and those things (including property) that surrounded him were his? This is a common problem with many Christians; they are not sensitive enough when God gives them something until God Himself puts it in their very hands. But God is tired of bringing everything to our doorsteps; He wants us to wake up as giants and exercise our rights as His children. Until now, Christians are still sleeping and unbelievers are taking over our birthrights. They climb up to the highest offices in every country. Some Christians are so naive and ignorant that when they first heard that they are a spirit living in a body, they think everything will happen and remain in the spirit. Till now some Christian sisters believe that their life partner will just appear in their prayer room like a lightning flash when they are in prayer and fasting. **The fact that you are a Christian does not mean you should be foolish**. Actually, the Bible says King Solomon was the wisest man who ever dwelt on the earth. You walk pass a Multibillion Company every day on your way to work, which is owned by a non-believer, and all you do is to admire it all the time. You've been working in this International Oil Company as a clerk for 20 years and all you do is you come to church every Sunday to thank God for giving you this job as the only black person in this company.

Come on brother, that Multi-billion Company is yours; hello sister, that International Oil Company is yours. Do you know why God placed you at that location? Don't be like Abraham and wait for years until God comes to you and say to your face: get up and go take it. Abraham was lucky God told him to do so but you may not be that lucky to receive that word from God simply because God is now staying in your inside in the form of the Holy Spirit. Please look around you and begin to see all the things that God has given you but you're still living in ignorance and weeping day and night. Do you think when God gave Canaan to the children of Israel; the land was lying bare and juicy? No, my sister, they had to fight all the people living on the land and took over from them. So it may actually happen that the Ferrari that your next door neighbor is using is yours according to God, but you'll have to rise up and work things out. The way you are, you sleep 10 hours in a day, work for only 6 hours in a day and chat with friends and colleagues for the remaining hours of the day. No, we don't receive the blessings of God just like that; you have to take more responsibility of your affairs before God can entrust you with the responsibility of such a big company. And it makes a lot of sense if you think of such a big company which provides for over 5000 families and you expect God to entrust the lives of all these families into the hands of a lazy person who can collapse the business in just one day? **Sometimes it is very important for you to qualify yourself before God can qualify you.** I'm quite sure that God did not have on His agenda to make Daniel a prophet initially, but when He saw his devotion to his people (the Jews) and God Himself, God decided to reveal Himself to Daniel. Daniel took the burden of the whole of Israel as his own burden and took it up to God in prayer. The way you are, all you think about is how to gain power and control affairs and you're expecting God to promote you and make you a leader of thousands of people. I do not mean you should put it in your mind that every good thing owned by your neighbor is yours but I want you to understand that God has given you the license to acquire a similar mansion like your neighbors' or even acquire a better one than theirs if only you intend to get those things to glorify the name of God. Sometimes we don't even acquire those things that we desire even if we pray and fast, simply because we may carry the wrong motives. Begin to realize who you are in Christ and arise! Enough of the weeping and the time wasting; start building your faith in the Lord, Jesus Christ. You've been a man of God for over 15 years and have kept 100 members for the past 15 years and all you do is to fight everyone in town who crosses your way and try to prove to them that you carry the oil of God. Come on Pastor, things have changed in our days; Joshua and the Israelites fought their enemies with swords but we have a modern way of fighting challenges as Christians. Go into your closet and begin to declare things that you want to see happen until they are established. Have you not read in your own Bible that *"your latter blessing shall surpass the former?"* – **Hagar 2:9**. Yes God is waiting for your church to reach out to 10 million people in the world and you are still busy fighting other men of God for taking your members. The Bible puts it nicely as:

"Go to the ant, you sluggard! Consider her ways and be wise, Which, having no captain, Overseer or ruler, Provides her supplies in the summer, And gathers her food in the harvest. How long will you slumber, O sluggard? When will you rise from your sleep? A little

sleep, a little slumber, A little folding of the hands to sleep – So shall poverty come on you like a prowler, And your need like an armed man."

Proverbs 6:6-11

Till now some people believe that they are failing to make it in life because of their low educational background so they have accepted their fate which was propagated by the devil. Others even say to themselves, after all, 'I'm only a woman.' Come on, delete that idea from your mind and listen, have you not read in the Bible that a woman by the name Deborah saved a nation as powerful as Israel when men were panicking and shaking like old women who were suffering from a partial stroke? – **Judges 4 & 5**. Arise and fix your marriage, you are a woman of valor, created in the image of God. Don't you know that the strength of your man is in your hand? You have a spiritual obligation to respect your husband but you're no inferior to him at this hour of need so quit discouraging yourself and save your family from the hands of the evil people who are waiting to see your downfall.

Arise, O Africa, Antarctica, Asia, Australia, Europe, North America, and South America,; mighty continents of the world; continents made with the strength of the sun and arm like the lion; you have been striving for years, but there is more to be done. Where are the brave, diligent and loyal citizens of your land? Today leaders kill each other in the quest for power; rob their own nations due to greed; abandon their own people and liaise with other people because of corruption? Let us quit wasting our own land and arise from our sleep. Let us stand as mighty men and women of valor and see how many lives we can save and the smiles that we can bring to our people. Let us quit fighting each other and begin to fight towards a common goal. Let us stop blaming our predecessors and start building now.

The reading from **Proverbs 6:6-11** said look for the ways of the wise and go learn from him. It's as simple as that. It's been decades since you probably started having problems as a nation. So far what have you done about it as a citizen (man or woman, young or old, educated or uneducated) and what have you done about the situation as a political leader? The Bible says look for a solution at all cost and don't wait for poverty to take over your whole land for it will hit you like a thief. I was made to understand that a nation like China once suffered from a severe turmoil and economic crisis but when the leaders and citizens made up their mind to work together to build their nation, God gave them the strength and they became successful. **It is never too late until you never start anything positive**.

2. The second lesson that I want us to learn from **Genesis 13:14-17** is the part that said: "*walk in the land through its length and its width, for I give it to you.*"

Many successful people will tell you that success does not come on a silver platter; you have to work for it even if God blesses you with it. Imagine God tells you to walk through the entire land of your country by its length and width; is it a simple task? Because God knew that Abraham could face challenges in life one day, he might as well think that maybe the land is probably not going to support him so he might go and look for a greener pasture somewhere else. So God told him to examine carefully the whole land and he will surely discover wealth in the same land which will eventually lead to his breakthrough. Most people have left the place of their breakthrough to other places where there is nothing left for them because of temporary challenges. The same thing happened in **Judges 11:3**. The Bible says a great man by the name Jephthah *"fled from his brethren and dwelt in the land of Tob, and worthless men banded together with Jephthah and went out raiding with him."* Just imagine a great judge of Israel running away from his own people to dwell with worthless or foolish people all because of some problems he experienced in the family. The Bible says when Jephthah returned to his people; he was chosen as the leader (president) of the whole Israel and fought a fierce battle which brought victory to the whole land; where they were set free from oppression. Our families, nations, continents, and the world are suffering because you and I are not there to take up our posts and set our people free from oppression and captivity like Jephthah did. Don't look at your present state and condemn yourself; refuse to listen to the names that people are calling you with. The Bible says you are a winner in Christ and you can do all things through Christ who gives you strength (**Philippians 4:13**).

As I explain further under point 2, God is encouraging us to be hardworking Christians for a lazy man will not eat. I will use this platform to appeal to my fellow Christians to start working hard towards their dreams because God will not come from heaven to implement the wonderful ideas that you have in your mind. You must first make an effort to put all your ideas on paper, study them, acquire the necessary knowledge in that area which you want to operate, edit and correct the initial plan and then implement them in real life. Do you remember that God didn't build the ark for Noah, rather He asked Noah to build the ark himself? Noah didn't complain that he wasn't an engineer or a carpenter but he listened to the voice of God. God said you are more than a conqueror and that is what matters.

I mean the fact that you are a baker does not mean that you cannot open and run a modern hospital for your people. All you need to do is to employ the people with the right expertise and you do the supervisory role. I'm telling you this for you to realize that there is no limit to your abilities as long as you remain in Christ. Laziness and success in life are serious enemies that cannot co-exist. As a man of God, there is nothing on this earth that is stopping you from working to generate income to support your family and the ministry. Don't hide behind the altar and tell the congregants that you are not working because you have been praying for them all day long. What moral lesson are you teaching your congregants? I have met some Christian brothers and sisters who think that it is okay to quit your school or work as long as you have been called or anointed by God. We must be very careful as spiritual leaders because whatever we do can affect our members positively or negatively. Man of God, you don't have to quit the work of God but you can remain as a man of God and still do business or create systems that can produce money to support your ministry and family. We also have the responsibility to teach our members to understand in practical terms when the Bible says faith without works is dead. We pray for God's blessings to be with us, and after that we go out to the fields to work hoping that God will give us a good harvest at work. I have never read from anywhere in the Bible where a certain anointed man or woman of God prayed so much to God and became so successful without putting their gifts to work. This means that as you believe God to make you become the best medical doctor in your region, you must also be prepared to study more about medicine and even pursue some professional medical courses that will enhance your knowledge. The way you are now, you have long given up studying any course related to Science and have never studied a course related to medicine in the past, yet you want to become a doctor. Let's say even if God could say go and head the best government hospital in your area, how are you going to fit? You need to acquire knowledge to pursue your dreams. We have seen many great people go to the grave poor without being able to implement their great ideas because they failed to acquire the right knowledge or seek appropriate help to implement their thoughts. You may be a housewife reading my book right now. Even though I would have loved for you to be actively working whilst you remain as a loyal and supportive wife to your good husband, but if for some reason you cannot do active work, for now, there is still more that you can do to earn extra income. The world has grown so much that today many people can work from home. For some, all that they need is a computer and access to the internet and they can make fortunes; some write stories and novels as their full-time job; some are freelancers; others are motivational speakers who go out only and when they have a presentation to make, etc. These are just a few examples, but there are many things that you can engage yourself in. You may be hospitalized because of a broken limb but you still have some energy to do something; you may be in the prison cells right now and you think your life has ended but I want to tell you that there are too many things that you can do to change your life and family right now. Think about it and please make a decision now or sooner. Do whatever you can at all cost not to remain idle for

Christ's sake. If you're thinking right now that I'm a babysitter and I'm supposed to be with the baby all the time, then I want to tell you that you're the most fortunate person on earth. Since your job does not demand so much brain work, you can have enough time to think about so many ideas and issues in life, including the writing of a book about the stages that children go through during the early stages in life. With your experience and knowledge, you can write a book about babies or babysitting that can earn you a fortune. All you need is determination and the realization of who you're in Christ. Don't forget that the fact that you bought yourself a nice car and built yourself a house does not make you a successful person on earth. **True success is contagious**. This simply means a truly successful person is the one who has lifted many others (not only their family members) up through the ladder of success.

Sometimes I get shocked to see how this same tongue that many abuse, and end up in trouble, others are able to tame theirs and train them such that they earn fortunes from speaking with no unique technology or expensive equipment involved. There are so many sources that we can pull wealth from so there is absolutely no reason why you should even remain poor for a day. This is the main reason why God has given you this wonderful book as a free gift to help you unlock your destiny in life.

From the following accounts:

Then God said, "Let Us make man in Our image, according to Our likeness; let them have dominion over the fish of the sea, over the birds of the air, and over the cattle, over all the earth and over every creeping thing that creeps on the earth."

Genesis 1:26

Then God blessed them, and God said to them, "Be fruitful and multiply; fill the earth and subdue it; have dominion over the fish of the sea, over the birds of the air, and over every living thing that moves on the earth."

Genesis 1:28

I would like to say that God has given dominion to man over all creation, living or non-living. With this information you don't have to waste time thinking about whether you're powerful than Satan or not; the answer is simple – **you are far powerful than Satan, the devil**. I know that the devil will not like it as you discover this truth so let me repeat it aloud, you are so powerful than the devil. And do you know why? The Bible just said we have been given dominion over every living thing that moves on the earth and the devil is no exception.

So even if you are going to forget about who you are, then please remember that you are powerful than the devil. The devil knows that you don't know this that is why he's taking advantage of you and manipulating you. Even as you have discovered this secret, you are still asking 'how' but your own Bible has said so. If you knew how powerful you are in Christ, you wouldn't give the devil any second of your life to destroy you. When man sinned against God, he lost his dominion and the devil rose up to destroy him but Jesus came down quickly to intervene by sacrificing Himself to restore the dominion back to man. Do you think if Jesus Christ could go to the extent of sacrificing Himself for us, then it will be difficult for Him to hand over the authority over the earth to us? No, He came because of that and that is the reason why He said after His resurrection that *"now all powers both in heaven and on earth have been given onto me; I therefore send you to go to all nations to preach the kingdom of God to them and I have given you power over sickness and all unclean spirit"* – (**Luke 9:1**). The unclean spirit in this context is the devil. Do you think if the devil couldn't defeat Jesus when He left all His glory and came as a human, then is it now that he can defeat Jesus, the King of kings and Lord of lords? Never! The Bible says Jesus lives right in your inside. This means if the devil can defeat you, then he can defeat Jesus too; which can never happen, unless you are not a true believer. The Bible says in **Isaiah 5:13**, "*Therefore my people have gone into captivity because they have no knowledge.*" This is the very reason why I want you to be fully conscious of who you are. You are not a failure; you're not poor; you're not a sinner; rather you're the righteousness of God. You're God's own chosen weapon to destroy the works of Satan.

What is it that you are going through in life that you're finding it difficult to come out? Is the devil causing you to panic? Sister, do not kill yourself over anything because what you carry right now is priceless. Don't you know that you even have power over death itself (**Matthew 10:8**)? So why do you allow the spirit of death to convince you to take out your own life? The power of the Holy Spirit in you can pay 10 times the price of whatever situation you might be going through right now. Brother, rise up and begin to rebuke the devil out of your life because if you can believe with me, you are quitting these drugs, smoking, and drinking right now! Our Savior Jesus Christ is taking care of all your bills, so please don't give up on Him; He's strengthening you right now as we speak. My dear mother, who is reading this book right now, there is nothing too big that our God cannot do okay? Is it about your husband or children? Go and ask Hannah, Sarah, Esther and Ruth and they'll say what God did for them and their families as well. Are you looking for a baby? Begin to declare that the Bible says none shall be barren (**Exodus 23:26**); I believe there is too much power in your tongue that can move mountains if only you can believe. Are you looking for a breakthrough in business? The Bible says in **Isaiah 48:17**, *"Thus says the Lord, your Redeemer, The Holy One of Israel: 'I am the Lord your God, Who teaches you to profit, Who leads you by the way you should go."*

Even as I come to the end of this chapter, I would like to refer you to the following Scripture:

"Arise, shine; For your light has come! And the glory of the Lord is risen upon you."

Isaiah 60:1

If you were waiting for the right time to do something good and bring about a great change in your life, family, and nation, then this is the right time to do it. Quit blaming only politicians and the wicked people in your town and start doing something that will bring about change. Sometimes the devil brings evil people around you just for you to waste all your useful time fighting them in the name of enemies. The day you will understand the revelation that vengeance belongs to the Lord and our weapons of warfare are spiritual but not physical, you'll go very far. That will be the day that you be able to see your destiny clearly and focus on your God-given abilities to bring about the change that you have been looking for all this while.

The above Scripture is, therefore, telling you to arise, shine; for your light has come! This is actually a command from God to you; asking you to rise up in your might and start changing your world. The Bible says you cannot light a lamp and put it under the bed, but instead, we put it in a place where it can shine brightly to give light to every corner.

Chapter 9

Remain Faithful unto God – Intimacy with God

I have seen many great men of God start very well and yet end up in a very miserable way. We're made to understand as Christians that it is the end that matters and not the beginning. God told Abraham that I am going to bless you so that you may tell your children and your children's children about Me. In fact, the Bible makes it so clear that He's a covenant keeping God. God told David that He shall preserve the seat of kingship for his descendants if only they are going to remain faithful unto Him. Unfortunately, when King Solomon, the son of David disobeyed God, God changed His mind and decided to remove the kingship from the house of David. I want you to understand that **every covenant comes with conditions**. If one party breaks the rule of the covenant, then the other party is free from whatever is binding him or her to the first party. This is why God said to the children of Israel in the Scripture:

"If you are willing and obedient, You shall eat the good of the land; But if you refuse and rebel, You shall be devoured by the sword."

Isaiah 1:18-20

You, therefore, have to be careful to respect the conditions of a covenant if you want to continue to reap the benefits of the covenant. We call God a covenant keeping God but the problem is do we keep our covenant with God faithfully? Throughout the Bible, from Genesis to Revelation, the Bible has stated clearly how God is going to reward His children if they remain faithful to Him.

Many anointed men of God have fallen spiritually because they failed to honor God at some point in their lives. This is why John said in the following Scripture:

"Remember therefore from where you have fallen; repent and do the first work, or else I will come to you quickly and remove your lampstand from its place – unless you repent."

Revelation 2:5

It is a pity that Christians do not respect the anointing any more in our days. We hear of cases where men of God consult satanic agents for diabolic powers to maintain their ministry. This is very demeaning and embarrassing but thanks be to God for the lives of His holy servants who have kept themselves pure till date. In the book of the Acts of the Apostles, the Bible records an incident where a Christian called Ananias and his wife

Sapphira died on the spot because they lied to the Holy Spirit. I want Christians to be very careful when dealing with God or the Holy Spirit because the consequences can be very grievous. Many Christians hide under the veil of grace to constantly sin against God but what I want you to understand is that what happened to Ananias and Sapphira happened in the days of grace. I have heard many Christians argue seriously that the grace of God has taken care of all our sins so no one person is condemned. In as much as the statement on its own appears to be correct, the practicality is that grace will not cover you if you remain in your sins. Grace is only put to use if we make the decision to live a holy life. In that case, what grace does is that instead of you to pay for all the sins you committed, the blood of Jesus pays every sin off so that you can start a new life in Christ. To put it in plain language, if the court condemns you to face a death sentence because of your offense, then you'll surely face the death penalty whether you repent of your evil act or not. But in the case of grace, the moment you genuinely repent, the death sentence is removed immediately from you and you are given a second chance to live a good life. If you want to live long, never let the fear of the Lord part from your heart. Many men and women of God who have lost God's touch on them is because of the lack of the fear of God. When God started using them mightily, they allowed pride to enter them. Grace is therefore not a license for you to keep on sinning against God because Ananias and his wife received judgment in the period of grace; so do not mock God on the grounds of grace. **Be serious with God so that He too can be serious with you**.

I, therefore, want to use this opportunity to teach you how to maintain your blessings, which ultimately came from God. Have you ever seen a waterfall that is cut from its source of supply? The moment that can happen, then the waterfall will cease from being a waterfall. The same principle applies to all Christians. **Psalm 124:8** says that *"Our help comes from the Lord, Who made heaven and earth."* From this verse, it is important for every Christian to note that everything that they possess comes from God and their life is completely dependent on God. This means that breaking away from God is an attempt to break away from your blessings and to possibly end your life. In order for you to continue to remain in Christ and He in you, the following things will be very vital:

1. Holiness

It is very important for you to remember that we are called onto holiness as Christians. We cannot claim to be disciples of Jesus Christ if we want to cling onto our past sinful life. Once you become a Christian, there is a separation between your past and your present. And the Bible confirms it with the words:

"If anyone be in Christ, then the old things are gone and he becomes a new creation in Christ"

We, therefore, have to live a clean and pure life if we want to walk with Christ faithfully. Holiness is not an act of becoming sober; it is an act of practicing your Christian faith as you follow the statutes of God. Holiness includes acts like an expression of love, kindness, self-control, alms-giving, caring for the needy, etc. It is not a matter of dressing in a white robe and joining your two hands in front of you like you are in prayer. It is something which is supposed to be part and parcel of our lives every day and we must not struggle to do it. We don't vacate on holiness as a child of God. We are not called onto holiness within the four corners of the church, rather we are called to live holy lives every second of our lives and to reach out to thousands of people in our schools, workplaces, communities and everywhere else with the beauty of holiness in us. And even as we minister onto others with our lifestyle, people may see our good deeds and give thanks to the Father, who is in heaven; and others may also be drawn onto Him.

2. The Word of God

Jesus said don't you know that a man must live by every word that proceeds out of the mouth of God? – **Matthew 4:4**. This means our survival as Christians depend on the Word of God. Not only does it fuel us in life, but it is also our life manual. A Christian who does not study and dwell in the Word of God is a powerless Christian. The only reason why it almost seems that every arrow that the devil throws on us hits us is that we don't dwell in the

Word of God. The Word is called the bread of life. Can you imagine yourself (not fasting) going to work every day and yet not eating any physical food continuously for one week? You will discover that your body will become too weak to support you to even carry out your routine duties effectively. If we were to care for our spirit the same way that we care for our physical bodies, the world was going to experience so much of the power of God. Let's assume that you got married to a wife who brought in her personal maid to assist her and from nowhere you begin to take very good care of the maid more than your own wife. Does it make sense? This is exactly what we are doing and yet we complain when things are not moving the way that we want. We know very well that the Bible says we are a spirit living inside a body. So my question is, the person (your spirit) and the body (house for your spirit), which is more important? If we can spend several hours to dress up this body before we walk out of our rooms, don't you think it is only fair to spend some time to study the Word at least every day, before we move out of our house and when we return home? It is high time Christians realize that studying the Word of God is not an optional matter; rather it is a requirement if you value your relationship with God and want to be victorious over your enemies. Do you remember I mentioned earlier that we as Christians are stronger than the devil? But we cannot defeat the devil easily like that without certain things in place. Go and ask the seven sons of Sceva; how they were beaten up by the devil? Christianity is a warfare, it is not a platform for experimentations, so we must understand it as such and attach all seriousness to it. The Bible says God created the whole universe with a spoken Word. It does not end there, the Bible also states it clearly that in the beginning was the Word, the Word was with God and the Word was God. Do you see the connection here? God is the Word and everything depends on Him. How privileged we are as Christians that He has offered Himself freely onto us in His Word and yet we don't value Him. How then do we expect God to intervene when we intentionally abandon Him (His Word) and later fall into problems? He said if you want to follow me, then follow My Voice because My sheep hear My Voice. How can we hear the Voice of God if not through the Word of God?

3. Prayer

Another way of keeping our relationship with God is by living a life of prayer daily. Prayer is a means by which we communicate with God. Even on a human level, it is only through effective communication by which we sustain our relationships, business, resolve our differences, give instructions, etc. Even Jesus, the Son of God had to pray all the time whilst He was here on earth. It was reported that when all the disciples were sleeping, He went up the mountain to pray alone for hours. There was a time that He asked the disciples that can't you stay with Me in prayer for at least one hour? This means Jesus Christ was a man who prayed a lot. I even remember when the Jews caught the woman in adultery and they brought her to Jesus, it was reported that whilst they were busy placing charges, Jesus bowed down in prayer. No one understood what He was doing; the only thing they saw was that He wrote on the ground with His finger. I am very certain that He was in deep prayer whilst they were making all the noise about the woman. Jesus was teaching us a very good lesson that we handle very big problems in life with prayer. One would say Jesus was God but how come He prayed all the times; He was giving us an example to follow as Christians, especially spiritual leaders in various churches. He was telling every man or woman of God to pray ten times more than your followers if you want to be able to win over all the physical and spiritual battles that your members may be going through. As a man of God don't get to the stage where you form a prayer team so you feel like you must just take a break from prayer or think you already have a heavy store of prayer bank so you can go on vacation. As a matter of fact, you must pray more than every member or leader in the church.

Most people take three square meals daily just to maintain their physical body so in a like manner I believe every Christian should make at least 3 times of prayer daily to maintain their spiritual well-being. These three sessions of prayer must be at least one hour for each session. In between these sessions you can have very short moments of prayers like 5, 10, 15 or 20 minutes throughout the day. If you can develop a routine prayer lifestyle you will begin to realize how much your life is going to change.

4. Fasting

"This kind can come out only by prayer and fasting"

Mark 9:29

Jesus told His disciples after they have failed to cast out an evil spirit from a person that this kind can only come out through prayer and fasting. We have to understand that just as it is required to take a balanced diet for the proper upkeep of our bodies, we also need a spiritual balanced diet. In as much as prayer is very good for a Christian, you can only become a rounded Christian if you can combine prayer with holiness, fasting, the Word of God and hard work. This means that if choose to depend only on prayers, you cannot see any results. I must say many Christians are of this attitude where they pray more than everyone else but they can't forgive their neighbor. Beloved if you want to please God, then you must balance your spiritual diet and that is when you will start to see results.

The Bible says though Jesus was the Son of God, yet he had to go through 40 days of prayer and fasting before He started His ministry here on earth. I want you to understand that prayer is not a substitute for fasting; they both work towards your spiritual growth. There are some cases that you may need fasting to supplement your prayer as Jesus advised His disciples. A time of fasting is a moment where you put your body to death and make your spirit more active in the Lord.

5. Hard work

I praise God for those Christian brothers and sisters who are already working hard to glorify the name of our Lord Jesus Christ. The Bible says a lazy man must not eat. It becomes too embarrassing to meet Christians who think they can make it by only prayer and fasting. I'm sorry to say that if you're like that, then you're wasting your useful life on earth as well as disappointing the God who made you. The Bible says God put Adam in the garden to tend and maintain it. Even though there was plenty of food in the garden, God did not tell Adam to be praying and fasting all day long; instead, He told him to cultivate the garden and keep it. He was responsible for seeing to the wellbeing of all the animals in the garden as well. **God hates idling and He expects us to be doing profitable work all the time.** Today we have men of God who even abandon their children in the house whilst they sit in the church all day long. They tell their families that they cannot make time with them because they have to pray for all the members. I'm sorry to say that your responsibility as a man of God includes your children, wife and your entire family. In fact, it is your responsibility to train your children with the correct moral values and bring them in the way of the Lord. Today the children of many men of God live a wayward life because of the lack of proper time management.

I'd, therefore, like to say that we all have a responsibility to take care of every task or assignment that God has given us and we can only achieve that through hard work and proper time management.

Now that you have become fully aware of the five points (Holiness, The Word, Prayer, Fasting and Hard work) that I explained as ways of maintaining your faith with God, it is now time for us to consider how we can practice all five of them effectively in order to achieve satisfaction and success in our Christian journey as well as to maintain an intimate relationship with God. I'd like us to concentrate on the connection between practicing your faith and building an intimate relationship with God. Today we have some Christians who are able to keep these five levels of faith practice, yet they are not able to touch the heart of God. An example of an intimate relationship with God in the Bible can be taken from the friendship between Abraham and God.

And the Lord said, *"Shall I hide from Abraham what I am doing, since Abraham shall surely become a great and mighty nation, and all the nations of the earth shall be blessed in him?"*

Genesis 18:17-18

In the Bible verse above, you should understand that it wasn't the case like Abraham was going to be in trouble that is why God wanted to warn him about it. It was a problem with his distant relative (nephew-Lot) and yet God thought it necessary to discuss it with Abraham first. A man like you and I through whom God could confide and listen to him on the spot. Let me ask you the simple question, how long does it take for your prayers to be answered? If your prayers are even answered at all, then it could probably take days, weeks, months or years. Now the case with Abraham was totally different, he had moved from the level of waiting for the heavenly protocol to record his personal details, put him on the waiting list and ask him to wait for the date of interviews. He had reached the level where the moment they see his call, they'll inform God immediately no matter how busy He might be. And when God asks His special assistant, who is on the line? The moment he answers, it's Mr. Abraham; God will be like, put him through immediately.

With the case of the destruction of Sodom and Gomorrah, the Bible says there were instant discussions and negotiations between God and Abraham. It wasn't an issue of waiting on God with prayer and fasting for 7 days. There was an open dialogue between the Creator and His creation. The initial plan of God was to totally destroy the land of Sodom and Gomorrah, but God was willing to compromise if Abraham could convince Him. Because Abraham had favor before God, he and God engaged in a long discussion and the two of them agreed that if the Angels find ten righteous people, then the land would be spared. This is the level of relationship that we need to build with God as Christians. We cannot claim to know God if we can't feel God's heartbeat and He cannot feel ours either. The Bible says because you have not listened to My voice, I will not rescue you when trouble hits you; you will call upon Me and I will not answer you. That's why the same Bible says call upon God when He's near. I want us to understand that there is order in God. Some Christians believe that they can do everything their own way and at the end come back to lean on God. It does not work that way. Christianity is a full-time calling, not a part-time calling. **Christianity is not the last option to make in life, it is the ultimate choice to make in life**. We have misunderstood the whole concept of Christianity and feel like we can do everything that we feel like doing and still enjoy the grace. As I said earlier, it was still the season of grace when Ananias and his wife Sapphira died (on the spot) so you must be very grateful to God that though you have committed a worse sin than that, you are still alive.

God is giving you a second chance to put your things in order.

I'll give you a few reasons why we're not able to touch the heart of God:

- though we can do everything for God; yet within our hearts, we don't place Him first. It does not matter how much offerings you can give in church or how long you can pray and fast; the main secret is **what value do we give to God**? Do we come first before Him? Or do your family members come before Him? The Bible says Jesus watched as everyone gave their offering but there was one particular offering that touched His heart than all; so He made the statement, *"this woman has given more than anyone"* (**Luke 21:3**). The people wondered because this was just a poor widow who even struggled to survive.

So when Jesus perceived what was in their hearts, He explained, that many people gave out of the abundance that they had, but this poor widow gave everything that she had. I'm not asking you to go and give out everything that you have, but I want you to understand that we have to think through carefully every act that we do before God because even though man sees from the outside, God sees from the inside. God judges our intention behind the act, not the very act.

The second example that I want to give you is the story of Job. Have you ever read this account and even reflected on it for about 45 minutes to understand how he probably felt on that day when all the bad news came to him within a short space of time? Now how did Job respond to the bad news?

"Then Job arose, tore his robe, and shaved his head; and he fell to the ground and worshipped. And he said: Naked I came from my mother's womb, And naked shall I return there, The Lord gave, and the Lord has taken away; Blessed be the name of the Lord.

Job 1:20-21

Did you hear that? A man who is greatly distressed for the loss of his 7 sons, 3 daughters, many servants, 500 yokes of oxen, 500 female donkeys, 7000 sheep, and 3000 camels all in one day suddenly entered into worship. Maybe you do not understand it yet, the Bible says Job was the greatest of all the people of the East; not only that, Job was a man who was blameless and upright before God. It was recorded; Job feared God and shunned evil. I'm not talking about an evil man who experienced a disaster, we talking about a holy man who pleased God so well. Now put yourself in the shoes of Job: how many people can still remember the name of God or can keep believing that God is real or even loves them in a time like this? Many would curse the name of God immediately and quit following Him. We need to be filled with a heart of worship all the time. The Bible says "rejoice always, again I say rejoice" – **Philippians 4:4**. Do you remember that Paul and Silas sang hymns whilst they were still in prison? Christians can be so soft that any small challenge they meet in life can cause them to renounce their faith. But we should remember that God can only put us to test in a time like that; to see how loyal and faithful we are to Him. Don't give up your Christian faith in challenging moments; it is actually the best time to prove to God about how much you love Him and how much you're willing to sacrifice for His sake. This is how we touch the heart of God. They say a friend in need is a friend indeed.

The third example I would like to give you is the story of Prophet Daniel.

"Now when Daniel knew that the writing was signed, he went home. And in his upper room, with his windows open toward Jerusalem, he knelt down on his knees three times that day, and prayed and gave thanks before his God, as was his custom since early days."

Daniel 6:10

Did you see what I just saw? This is the highest level of spirituality. Now Daniel was appointed as governor in Babylon and he performed so well more than all the other governors so they became jealous of him. Before I explain my main point, I want to bring to the attention of my readers, especially Christians who isolate themselves completely from politics and allow only non-believers to run the affairs of their country. It will actually be God's delight to see His children in higher government positions so we must not leave politics in the hands of only non-believers. It is the desire of God that good people should rule a nation, and Christians are no exception. Now the other governors convinced the king to sign a decree that no one should pray to any god for a particular period of time, having in mind that

Daniel would fall for it. So the penalty for disobeying the decree was for you to be fed to hungry lions. Come to think of it, Daniel knew their entire plot against him, yet he couldn't stay a day without his usual prayers where he communicated with God. The problem with many Christians is that when they read the Bible, they see it as a mere story but everything in it is real. Now many would think that one has to use 'common sense' when confronted with a case like Daniel's, especially if you know about their hidden agenda. Why must you be fed onto hungry lions when you could go without open prayer for just that period of time? Most of us apply too much 'common sense' in our service to the Lord, just to minimize problems and risks pertaining to our faith. Who knew if Daniel had made a vow with

God that he would make open prayers three times every day? Daniel's action could have been questionable and debatable if he had not made a vow to God concerning his routine prayers. In that case, as a practicing Christian, you have to live up to your promise and refrain from the use of 'common sense'. This is what we mean by the fear of the Lord. Another man in the Bible did the same thing when he made a vow to God that he would sacrifice whatever comes out of his house to meet him when God gives them victory over their enemies. God heard about the vow and he granted victory to Israel so Jephthah had no choice but to sacrifice his only daughter because she was the first person to come out to meet him (**Judges 11:34**). Dear reader, I want to take you to another level of faith where you'll learn to fear

God than anything that you can ever imagine. **It is better to die in the hands of God through a promise you made to Him than to die in the hands of Satan**. If Christians today understand this level of the fear of God, then we wouldn't go behind God to prostitute, take bribes, dupe our neighbors, render unfair treatment, compromise, etc. all in the name of seeking for survival or living out our heart desire at the expense of God's will for our lives. When vows and covenants are involved, please try as much as you can to desist from the temptation of 'common sense'. A practical example is if you promise God that you would give Him $50000 this month if He should bless you with that much or more and He gives you, please honor your word. The temptation comes in if in that same month your son is admitted in ICU and the doctors tell you that in order for your son to be revived, you have to pay an amount of $50000 for medication. What will you do in a case like this? My answer is simple: honor your word to God and leave the rest in His care. In any case, no one forced you to make that promise to God. If Daniel and Jephthah feared God enough to keep their word to Him, then you too can do the same.

My last example on this point is the story of Abraham. In **Genesis 22**, God told Abraham to sacrifice his only son, Isaac, and indeed the man got ready to do just that. In fact, I have never seen such kind of boldness and loyalty ever before in my life. Abraham was not supposed to do that as a form of sin offering to ask God's forgiveness for a crime he committed but it was a request from God. In fact, if God had asked you the same question, you might say to God in the face, get behind me Satan for it is written: "do not murder." You'll actually end up lecturing God on what is written and what is not in His own Word. Do you think you can go behind your wife secretly and go kill your only son? You won't! In fact, you will be the first person to disclose your discussion with God to your wife, thinking very well that she will refuse so that you can have an excuse to tell God. Exactly like what Adam did, you will tell God that you were willing to obey Him but your wife refused to give you the child. I hope you are taking note of the main revelation behind this discussion? Abraham understood this principle so when he was confronted with the difficult situation of sacrificing his only dear son to God, he did not resist. He was willing to honor God and then suffer the consequences later. This could have resulted in the termination of his marriage or he could have ended up in prison. The question is, who do you seek to please first: yourself, wife, child, friend, parent, wealth or God?

- The second reason why we are not able to touch the heart of God is an issue of faith. **Faith is the most important ingredient to transform the spiritual into physical**. I understand that we have different kinds and levels of faith, but I'll not be talking about that. Without classifying it, one kind of faith that you can use to enter into the supernatural is the type of faith that Jesus spoke about:

"If you have faith as a mustard seed, you will say to this mountain, Move from here to there, and it

will move; and nothing will be impossible for you."

Matthew 17:20.

Mountain, as used in this context, can represent any problem or difficult situation that you are trying to solve. This is the kind of faith that sees the results even before you declare it. This faith knows no fear and it does not accommodate alternatives- it solely depends on one answer only e.g. if you want the blind to see, then you want just that; you will not accept any 1 million USD to support this blind person in replacement of his healing. You want sight restoration for him and nothing less, nothing more – no negotiations. Here you don't mind as a man of God that the whole congregation will remain in church praying until the next Sunday still praying on the same topic (no food, no bath, and nothing). I call this kind of faith crazy faith. **It is the type of faith where you disturb heaven until heaven realizes that you are indeed an asset in the Kingdom so they'll rather answer your prayer immediately before they lose you.** In this faith you don't care about the people surrounding you as to whether it will happen or not; all you see is God and the solution. If you can get a revelation on this faith, there will be absolutely nothing that you cannot achieve here on earth. The Bible says the Prophet Elijah put his head between his thighs and prayed. What kind of prayer is this where you put your head in between your thighs? I can tell you that it was a crazy prayer, where the man was prepared for nothing else but rain because he heard the voice of God that there will be rain. How many times has God given you a prophecy of your life that you shall not die and yet you are still afraid? The Bible says you shall not lack, yet you literally beg to survive and you call yourself a Christian. Come on my sister, become angry at the devil and use your faith to claim what is rightfully yours. The situation you find yourself in is not pleasant and it is only you who understands it better. Quit fighting your husband or wife and start putting your faith to work. Declare things and start going out for them. Do you still remember that Jesus paid the price for everything that you're looking for today? The Bible says Elijah prayed for the first time and there was no rain but he did not quit. The good thing he did was that whilst he was praying he was still checking the clouds for visible signs of the rain. This is what we call miracle enforcement. The mustard seed's faith demands instant results so before you approach the scene you should have sufficient power to complete it. Even if you don't see the results immediately, you don't doubt in your heart because you know that it shall surely happen. Now many people declare things during prayer but the bad thing is that they don't work towards it or even wait for it. If you have prayed to God to help you to acquire a scholarship to travel outside your home country to study your PhD, then you cannot afford to tell me that one year down the line you still do not have a passport or a research topic but you're still anxiously waiting for your prayer to be answered. It does not work that way. You pray and you also implement things physically to prove to God that you know what you are doing and you mean business. Elijah prayed and checked for the first time but there was no rain, he did the same thing the second time, but there was no rain, he repeated it over and over again for the seventh time until he saw a sign of rain. This is a combination of determination, faith, action, and perseverance. If you have been praying so hard to God expecting a very big breakthrough and God grants you a smaller breakthrough to test your faith, don't despise it, rather see it as a sign of the answer to your bigger breakthrough. Elijah encouraged himself with the sign of a cloud as small as the size of a man's hand. And guess what he told Ahab? He did not say I think it might rain, but he said in **1 Kings 18:44**, *"Go up, say to Ahab, 'Prepare your chariot, and go down before the rain stops you.'"* There was no rain yet when he uttered those words but he was 100% certain that the Word of God cannot fail. This is what we call exercising your faith. Do you know what it means if his word had not come true? Imagine telling a whole president to take a certain drastic decision that could possibly affect all the citizens and it turns out bad? Christianity is not as simple as some people see it; it involves risking your own life for what you believe in. But the good news is that our God is always faithful to those who faithfully stand out for Him. Don't give up too easily because they rejected your first application, do this application over and over again until you're approved; don't give the devil an option to make decisions on your behalf, you're a king and a champion in Christ.

- Another important thing to note as a Christian is that, you should always remember and understand that it is your season to rule and take over. I understand that many Christians are still waiting for their prayers to be answered by God, which is a good thing, but I want you to understand that it is not all prayers that we have to ask God; otherwise, we might wait for a pretty long time before we can find answers. As a matter, of fact God is also waiting for us to cause changes for Him to celebrate us as His children, so the problem is whilst we are waiting for God, God is also waiting for us; which means we can end up waiting forever. Do you think it is God's will that all your sons must die and now you are on the sick bed about to die, yet you are a faithful evangelist and a great ambassador in Christ? My brother, rise up on your feet and declare Esther's fast, pray in new tongues like a crazy dog and chase the devil out of your house. This kind of prayer does not need God's permission because God has already commanded us to cast the devil out of our midst. This is the stage where you've got to declare that if I die I die! After all, you are already dying anyway so what have you got to lose? Don't be too nice with the devil, he's inflicting pains on you because of your mindset; he knew that you'd blame God for your problems and would not look for a solution. The Bible says, on the last day people will see how small the devil was and say, so this was the man who caused the whole earth to tremble like that? The Bible says in **Isaiah 60:1** Arise, shine for your light has come. My question is what are you waiting for if you're not already shining? There is no need to keep on wasting time, blaming God, blaming people and blaming yourself. I know that you have exhausted all your energy and tried every option but rise up as a soldier in Christ and do it again. Sometimes all you need is a prophetic word from the Lord and you can find success using the same old approach. Peter didn't have to go back home to do some Advanced Diploma before he could make the bounty catch, he only had to obey the word of the Lord Jesus Christ. Jesus had asked him to repeat the same thing which he did before and he did not refuse or complain that I'm tired of doing the same thing over and over again. This is why the Bible says obedience is better than sacrifice. This is the right moment for you. To the young people and teenagers, it is not too early for you to start planning your life. Brazil's World Pele made his first World Cup's appearance at the age of seventeen. To the old people, you're not too old for you to make a decision to turn your life around, as well as your family and community. The founder of Kentucky Fried Chicken (KFC), Harland David Sanders opened his first franchise at the age of 62. Some say life begins at 40 but I don't believe so; life begins the moment you make the decision to fight and overcome all obstacles in life with the sole intention of improving your life, your family and the people around you. This is to say that if a young man at the age of 12 can see clearly the pattern of life he believes can bring about positive change to him and his entire family and he begins to pursue his dreams with all seriousness and devotion, then his life has already started at 12. It is not enough to be financially sound and yet be spiritually weak or physically unfit. When you read your Bible very well, you will understand that Jesus brought us life in abundance, thus life in all areas of life. You can't tell me that you are a prayer warrior and yet have been struggling financially for so many years. As a Christian you should be doing well in all areas of life: spiritually, financially, marriage, health, etc. This is what we call living Scripture since the Bible says we should be doers of the Word and not hearers.

Chapter 10

The Simple Life Model of Success

I have never met even one single person on this earth who's not passionate about success. Success is the vocabulary of everyone's mind right now. Whether you're a student, a minister of God, an employee, an employer, a footballer or whatever your profession may be, you obviously want to be successful. You may be calm and introvert in your approach to things, but that does not mean that you don't want to be successful in life. I, therefore, find it very important to address this issue of success so that all my readers can understand the key to success in their lives. I am very much convinced that if you can apply the principles explained in this model, then your life will never be the same after today. The moment we hear of success, people get so excited and anxious to know what's on the table because people are looking for definite and straight forward ideas to immediately implement and start making money. For example, if I can give you the financial position of ABCD Company, you may show interest in the company depending on the stability and how much profit the company is making per annum. With a proven track record and a good financial position, if ABCD Company should be selling a franchise, then many investors would be interested in that because with this business opportunity everything is detailed out clearly from the beginning. I must say this can be a great business idea if only you can afford it. My main concern is, no matter how much money one can get as a profit margin from such a franchise, not too many people can afford to buy the franchise. Many people are of the view that you can never rise to the top if you don't have any financial base but I totally disagree with that notion. So I have decided to introduce this model to everyone who really wants to make it to the top but is greatly stranded and does not know what to do again. Some are saying but we don't know anyone at the top management so how can we enter and become part of such a prestigious company?

Dear reader, the answer is very simple if you follow this model you will make it to the top. The Bible says I can do all things through Christ who gives me strength. When you read this Scripture, what comes into your mind? The Bible didn't say you can do some specific things, but it clearly stated that you **can do ALL things** through Christ who gives you strength. That means you can come from the poorest village in your community but if you desire to become the richest man in the world one day and you indeed work towards becoming that, then you can surely become. This can be confirmed from the Scripture below:

So he said to Him, "O my Lord, how can I save Israel? Indeed my clan is the weakest in Manasseh, and I am the least in my father's house."

Judges 6:15

This is one huge challenge that thousands of people are facing today. As a person, you may think you know yourself too well more than any other person. You may be right but you cannot know yourself so much than how much God knows you. It's very interesting to find Gideon arguing with the Angel of the Lord, all in the name of trying to justify his incompetence for the task God was giving him. Millions of Christians are suffering today because they think certain kinds of tasks are reserved for a certain group of people with special abilities. The family or village that you come from does not matter to God. The Bible says a man sees only the outside of a person but God sees what is inside the heart of a man. So God chose David over all his well-educated, great and very handsome brothers. So I want you to stop concentrating on your weaknesses and past experience and get ready to embrace the life that God has prepared for you. Follow the simple model below carefully and put it to practical use and you'll never regret it. I wish you the best of luck in the pursuit of all your plans with the help of God's power and sound principles to rise to the top.

Kodom's Model of Success in Life

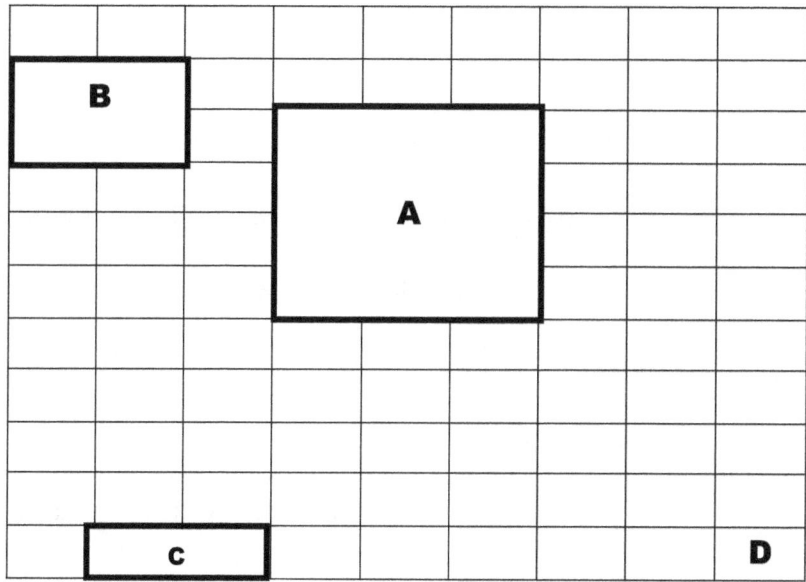

There are 112 blocks in total. These blocks represent businesses and business opportunities. The size of the blocks represents how successful the organization is doing. Block A is assumed to be the most successful business in the world.

Now the question is if you are at position D or E, how can you get to position A and experience a breakthrough in life?

- E is a place where you find yourself totally confused and doing absolutely nothing whereas point D is a position where you find yourself working, but at the same time, you're not making much from your work.
- The following actions are required in order to get to the top:

1. Discover how you can add value to an existing system

A system could be an idea or a business organization that is doing well already. The common culture that companies use to employ people is by inviting people to interview for a particular task within the organization.

Different companies use different approaches to recruit staff, which are mainly based on qualification and practical hands-on experience in the field being advertised.

One effective way of gaining recognition in a reputable company is by **conducting a thorough study about the operations of the company and discover** what you can bring on board in order to add value to the company. This is a time-consuming process that needs strategic thinkers with a definite objective on what they want to achieve. In this case, you see yourself as someone who is already working for the company from afar. Occasionally meet with some of the workers to collect all the necessary data to help you with your study. If it means signing up for an internship for a period of time, then you must go for it. On a more general note, some individuals or companies can present a proposal to another company to render certain kinds of services. This particular task goes beyond just sending a proposal about what kind of services that you render to similar companies. This particular task makes you study thoroughly what goes on in this particular company. Many people who work in an organization work because they have to earn a living from their work but you may assume the position of the CEO and an employee at the same time. You give a critical view of the whole organization and then pursue the interests of the organization. One important thing that I recommend before you embark on this task is that you must select a company that provides services relevant to your expertise, talent or interest. The main reason why is that the process is time-consuming and too demanding so if it is not in line with your passion, then you may give up too easily along the line. One huge advantage of this task is that even as you build yourself and acquire the relevant knowledge concerning the operations of the company, you are not just waiting for nothing; you also end up adding more value to your career or field of interest. If your research goes well, without necessarily joining that very company, you might be able to start a similar organization in the future.

2. Find just one problem to fix

Companies all over the world are looking for people who can provide a real-time solution to sign multi-dollar contracts with them. Many of the people who are employed generally possess "common" skills which may not be sufficient to solve some major and unusual problems. It is true that there is a huge challenge with employability but companies will pay anything to get hold of a person with extraordinary skill.

All you need to do is to find time to identify one major problem which the organization is facing and see how you can fix it. There is no one single company without any challenges, so look for at least one loose spot within the organization and research about how to solve that particular problem. As long as that solution can provide a facelift to the organization, they will appreciate your contribution more than the services of 1000 employees within the same organization. This means that you can be hired as a special consultant where you will be paid with huge sums of money set by your own terms and approval.

3. Creating a new model from studying an existing model

I really have a problem with people who tell me that they are just doing nothing. You can't afford to idle about as a Christian; God expects you to be working all the time, except if you decide to go on retirement or on pension. The fact that you can't find a job around does not mean you should remain idle. In fact, you can find a great opportunity to do something great if you're not working actively for any company. I believe that this will be the right time for you to organize your thoughts and create something on your own.

All you've got to do is by taking time to identify what kind of creation or field that you're passionate about. Then find an organization that does something similar to what you plan doing and study the model that they are using to help you understand your own model better. Innovation and inventions do not come from the sky, they start from the things that we are familiar with and how best we can put those things to effective use. Read more books about the idea, inquire from experts, gather more information and make yourself a private researcher. Don't wait for another company to employ you as a researcher before you start putting your knowledge to use. Work along with experts in the field and even bring some of them on board where necessary. Do your market studies very well and just make sure that your product or services carry the solution that people and companies need. Governments, institutions and private donors are looking for many viable projects to sponsor and support.

4. Start an entirely new project

Many great ideas die prematurely because the bearers of the ideas face one or two obstacles on the way and eventually quit or leave it unattended to for a while. As I said earlier, it is even a great opportunity for you if you do not have an active contract or obligation with any organization. In your mind, you may think that you are not working but that is the right time to discover an opportunity in life. Take your time and study your environment, study your community and begin to think about what you can do to improve the lives of people. I understand that some projects are capital intensive, and that is the main problem faced by young entrepreneurs right now, but I can tell you that sometimes you can start a multi-billion company without a dime if only you can package your thoughts very well and know who will be interested in the project. A couple of weeks ago, a young man walked into my office to ask for a short time to have a word with me. I initially did not want to pay attention to him but I later decided to give him only five minutes of my time. He explained a proposal to me and how he needed my help. After listening to him, I realized that I was interested in the project and I was even willing to provide some special services that could cost him so much money to bring life to the project without asking him to pay anything. There and there, the main financial burden of this young man was lifted, and not only that, but I was also willing to connect him to other stakeholders who could support the other stages of the project. My point is if you can present your well-packaged proposal to the right people, you may not have to worry about where to get the capital to start the project. **Innovative and constructive ideas can be converted into capital**.

5. Team up with the right people

I have seen many young graduates moving about, from one office to the other with their files in their hands looking for jobs. Some may do this for five consecutive years without any lack on their side. There is nothing wrong to be so determined in order to get the job that you desire. Some actually end up so disappointed after a reasonable number of trials and even give up on their careers or dreams. I like the saying, "Necessity is the mother of invention."

It is very important for people to begin to realize that they can team up together, pull their strengths and resources together and start a multi-billion company with hard work, trust, dedication, and commitment. Begin to brainstorm and identify the people who may possess the skills that you need and speak with them about your plans to start an organization. Document everything regarding how the organization will run, agreement policies, sustainability plans, and others. Remember that every single company that we respect today started so small like that until their dream became a reality.

11 years back, I met a group of five friends who were desperately looking for teaching jobs right after they graduated from the University. They searched all over but it was difficult to get a job. Lucky enough, these

friends studied different Majors in the University and one of them had a big apartment that could be used to start a Private School so I proposed to them to think about starting their own school but they refused because they were so much obsessed about getting employed. Years later, some of them came back to tell me that they wish they had taken my advice because the jobs they're now doing is not giving them the opportunity to grow and build students the way they had dreamt of initially. I am glad they are all working now, but the problem is none of them is satisfied with their job; some are still part-time teachers, others are full-time teachers but are not making anything to write home about. It sometimes pays to make certain decisions in life even if it'll take a little while for your plans to be realized. Don't be so quick to start work because you are looking for survival; take your time to plan your whole life; what you want to do, where you want to end and how you plan to do it even before you launch out. Don't follow what the masses are doing; you are completely different and unique in your own ways. **Think big and think possible**.

References:

1. The Holy Bible, NKJV
2. LiveScience at

   https://www.livescience.com/32437-why-are-250-million-sperm-cells-released-during-sex.html
3. Quote from Martin Luther King Jnr.

Thank you for finding time out of your busy schedule to read through this book. God bless you.

KINDLY LEAVE A POSITIVE REVIEW FOR THIS BOOK ON AMAZON IF YOU FIND THIS MATERIAL HELPFUL.

https://www.amazon.com/s?k=B07P89XP6M&ref=nb_sb_noss

Thank you

www.ingramcontent.com/pod-product-compliance
Lightning Source LLC
LaVergne TN
LVHW041249080426
835510LV00009B/658